The Dramaturgy of Performing Science

This is a concise survey of new play projects that bring together the worlds of science and performance and the benefits that dramaturgical praxis can bring to both disciplines.

Three approaches common to both performance and science – collaboration, experimentation, and interpretation – are reflected in a series of case studies that demonstrate the ways in which dramaturgical tools can inform the wider public about scientific knowledge and practice, provide a truly reciprocal model of cooperation in collaboration that happens early on in the research process, and inspire the creation of new dramatic forms that enact, rather than translate, the dynamics of scientific research.

Part of the *Routledge Focus on Dramaturgy* series, this is a vital account of collaborative work for scholars and practitioners of theater and performance, as well as readers across the sciences.

Jules Odendahl-James is a freelance director and dramaturg and from 2014 to 2024 was the director of academic engagement for the arts and humanities at Duke University, USA.

Focus on Dramaturgy

Series Editor: Magda Romanska

The Focus on Dramaturgy series from Routledge - developed in collaboration with TheTheatreTimes.com – is devoted to the craft of dramaturgy from multiple contemporary perspectives. This groundbreaking comprehensive series is authored by top professionals in the field, addressing a variety of current hot topics in dramaturgy.

The series is edited by Magda Romanska, an author of the critically-acclaimed Routledge Companion to Dramaturgy, dramaturg, writer, theatre scholar, and Editor-in-Chief of TheTheatreTimes.com.

Dramaturgy of Migration
Staging Multilingual Encounters in Contemporary Theatre
Edited by Yana Meerzon and Katharina Pewny

Diversity, Inclusion, and Representation in Contemporary Dramaturgy
Case Studies from the Field
Edited by Philippa Kelly

Dramaturgy of Form
Performing Verse in Contemporary Theatre
Kasia Lech

The Dramaturgy of History
Tom Bryant

Dramaturgy of Sex on Stage in Contemporary Theatre
Edited by Kate Mulley

The Dramaturgy of Performing Science
New Work in Interdisciplinary Contexts
Jules Odendahl-James

For more information about this series, please visit:
https://www.routledge.com/performance/series/RFOD

The Dramaturgy of Performing Science

New Work in Interdisciplinary Contexts

Jules Odendahl-James

LONDON AND NEW YORK

First published 2025
by Routledge
4 Park Square, Milton Park, Abingdon, Oxon OX14 4RN

and by Routledge
605 Third Avenue, New York, NY 10158

Routledge is an imprint of the Taylor & Francis Group, an informa business

British Library Cataloguing in Publication Data
A catalogue record for this book is available from the British Library

Library of Congress Cataloging-in-Publication Data
A catalog record has been requested for this book

ISBN: 9780367714352 (hbk)
ISBN: 9781032790237 (pbk)
ISBN: 9781003150848 (ebk)

DOI: 10.4324/9781003150848

Typeset in Times New Roman
by Taylor & Francis Books

This book is dedicated to Kelly, always.

And to Linden, who is my hope for the future.

Thanks to my parents, who provided my first experiences of how the arts and the sciences can work together.

Contents

Introduction

Of Forms and Formulas

To Reveal and Create

In the introductory chapter to his 1925 book *The Science of Playwriting*, lawyer and playwright Moses Malevinsky presents an extended survey of narrative and dramatic theorists. Quoting extensively from Barrett H. Clark's 1918 anthology *European Theories of the Drama* among other sources, he searches for terms like "formula," "technique," and "laws" to uncover the structure for dramatic writing. Malevinsky expresses disappointment in these sources' lack of "a consecutive formula, nor may one find an analytical or truly comprehensive definition of – a *play*" (6). By contrast, he will provide a "guiding compass" for theater informed by his work in the emerging field of copyright law. To that end, Malevinsky drafts "The Algebraic Formula" for plays: an emotion-rooted action "limited to approximately two hours" centered on "*one* theme, *one* central character, *one* plot" (110).[1] He argues that a play's "organic structure," comprises a "concentrated exposition of character in action, mental or physical, against seen and/or known and/or unseen and/or unknown forces" (107). Having won a 1925 copyright case (*Simonton v Gordon et al.*) by proving a successful play, *White Cargo*, was an uncredited adaptation of an earlier novel, *Hell's Playground*, Malevinsky presents The Algebraic Formula as the means to assess a play's essential qualities and the boundary between one artist's work and another's: "Not every play need necessarily be well made or closely knitted, but it must, by definitive processes (attained either scientifically, subconsciously or instinctively) be presented in such form as the masses of the people may understand and grasp" (108–9). Perhaps when Malevinsky employed The Algebraic Formula less successfully in a 1929 plagiarism case (*Nichols v Universal*), he realized the irreducibility of artistic expression to its structural components alone.[2] Writers and theorists

DOI: 10.4324/9781003150848-1

might invoke the language of science to describe key dynamics behind a script's composition, but the relevance often remains at the level of metaphor and a script's success or failure in production introduces factors less obedient to universal laws, quantification, and rationality.

Nonetheless, students and scholars still pursue empirical rules by which to create and evaluate theater. For example, a dramaturg's role within a production has been described as "fixer" or "script doctor," someone with specialized knowledge to be applied to an object toward its better, ideal functioning (Proehl 132–33). Dramaturgy as "the theory and practice of drama," originates with Gotthold Ephraim Lessing (1729–81), a playwright and influential drama critic. Lessing, somewhat like Malevinsky, presented his skills of analysis and assessment as a service to the public and the profession at a moment when the possibilities and proprieties of theater were changing. Lessing's ideas regarding dramatic form and their use in new play development became more widely influential after his death. He is credited with imbuing the role of the dramaturg with desirable traits: a theater artist with a unique depth of knowledge regarding theatrical form and aesthetic innovation, who helps examine a play's effectiveness and anticipated reception.[3] Contemporary dramaturgs continue to navigate the spaces between empirical ways of knowing often associated with science and the assumed boundless imagination of artistic creation.

This book explores this crux between the art and science of theater, focusing on a specific subgenre: theater about/of/with science. To engage this subject necessitates some acknowledgment of C.P. Snow's notion of Art and Science as the "two cultures"[4] ever in tension. Theater historian Kirsten Shepherd-Barr, a foundational scholar of science theater, notes how much each field "borrow[s] from one another for metaphoric explanations of what they are and what they do" (2020, 1). In her introduction to the *Cambridge Companion to Theatre and Science*, she argues that the notion of "Theater as laboratory" presents a long-standing, productive "common ground" between science and performance (4). The intertwined domains of theater and medicine have been well documented, perhaps most frequently in discussions of the operating theater, anatomical teaching and learning practices, and the freak show where bodily display and the performance of self that might counter or complicate a medical narrative offers an early vision of performance art.[5] Theater theorist Sue-Ellen Case, in her 2007 book *Performing Science and the Virtual*, notes the historical use of performance practices on and beyond the theatrical stage to "locate and define the scientific discoveries of their times" via "strategies of representation" that blur the "immaterial and material" (2). The "virtual" in her reading is not simply an outcome of digital technology innovations but a concept historically rooted in notions of effect, appearance, and potential, all elements central to theatrical performance as well as to "moral philosophy, optics, physics, and ontology" (3).

My interests in this arena of theatrical work began in the early 2000s after many years exploring the visual dramaturgy of forensic science depicted in popular culture, particularly serial television. There, the lab tools of many scientific fields (e.g., chemistry, anatomy, physics, psychology, engineering) are presented as quasi-independent actors, solving crime by uncovering a criminal's hidden motives.[6] Lab reports offer a new kind of deus ex machina, appearing at the critical moment with irrefutable material evidence and prompting a confession. Beyond the forensic frame, I began investigating visual and performance artists who engaged the worlds of biological and material sciences. I found scientists with artistic practices and scientists who employed visual or sonic tools such as microscopy, radiology, geographic information system (GIS) mapping, and data modeling to capture, depict, and articulate the representational elements of their research. I also noticed a growing strain of new plays and critically acclaimed productions of historical plays that dramatized scientific discoveries and scientist biographies. These seemed to parallel a new push for STEAM (**S**cience **T**echnology **E**ngineering and **M**ath or STEM + Arts) curricula in secondary schools and undergraduate liberal arts institutions.

The chapters that follow review science theater and performance projects since the mid-2000s, examining engines of new science play development in the United States, higher education's interdisciplinary dynamics around STEAM collaborations from which new work may spring,[7] and postdramatic and performance art experiments that construct research playgrounds out of scientific fields, techniques, and technologies. Thinking dramaturgically about plays inspired by science, about research collaborations forged between artists and scientists, and about the wide range of performance experiences they create provides new conceptions for interdisciplinary collaboration beyond the question of whether art serves science or science serves art. Dramaturgy, a practice of excavating histories and incubating possibilities, is a field uniquely positioned to curate and catalyze shared principles and bring the work of scientists and theater artists into compatible synergy even as our social authority and value remains disparate.

Facts and Truth

In his 1959 address best known for articulating the "two cultures" concept, physicist C.P. Snow presented an array of binary oppositions (Ideal vs. Real; Mind vs. Body; Nature vs. Culture) about whether phenomena are *found* or *made*, whether knowledge is *objective* or *subjective*, whether meaning is *inherent* or *constructed* (23, 33). While writers tend to invoke the "two cultures" as Art and Science broadly, Snow's construct focused on literary academics and radical poets, whom he characterized as conservative and backward-looking compared to physicists and engineers post–Manhattan Project, who were future directed and innovation oriented. Ultimately, Snow asserts a both/and conceptualization of knowledge as simultaneously found and made and points toward opportunities for interdisciplinary collaboration across the sciences and humanities. Science philosopher Thomas Kuhn and sociologist Bruno Latour each elaborated Snow's call. In *Structure of Scientific Revolutions* (1962) Kuhn cautions the reader to not mistake the science textbooks' presentation of a linear, positivist progression of scientific experimentation and discovery for reality. The rationality and objectivity of science are not given; they are constructed structures and practices:

> The existence of this strong network of commitments – conceptual, theoretical, instrumental, and methodological – is a principal source of the metaphor that relates normal science to puzzle-solving. … In these and other respects a discussion of puzzles and of rules illuminates the nature of normal scientific practice.
>
> (42)

Similarly, Latour (1987) argues in *Science in Action* that science is a force in society, not because of its inherent factualness but because of the networks circulating among scientific processes and products. It avoids incoherence through scientific methods that are evaluated by "the number of points linked, the strength and length of the linkage, the nature of the obstacles" (201). Kuhn and Latour helped forge a new field, Science Technology Studies (STS), inviting scholars to interrogate and intervene in the art-science binary, challenging assumptions regarding evidence, experimentation, and knowledge production. This line of reasoning regarding science as truth might be familiar to theater artists regarding discussions of realism as a *form* of theater not the a priori condition of theatrical representation itself.

STS scholars pull back the curtain on the dynamic processes of scientific inquiry and note external social pressures on the field and its practitioners that shape those dynamics. They do not, however, promote the adjudication of scientific findings by nonexperts. Only scientists hold authority over the meanings of scientific inquiry, but the drive to articulate generalizable rules does not mean absolutism: "Science aims for refined degrees of confidence, rather than complete certainty" (Reproducibility and Replicability 32). Journalists, the wider public, and even some scientists, however, can confuse absolutism with what science historian Naomi Oreskes (2017) calls "organized, [collective] scrutiny." Scientists create and test hypotheses to explain phenomena, particularly those not readily observable without technological assistance whether via microscope or mathematical model. They assert facts based on these measures rendered from and tested through the application of formulas and equations and their reproducibility to produce the same results. Artists might employ facts toward a goal of illuminating truths grounded in the deeply affectual realm of subjective experience. Art engages emotion, temporality, and perception as key attributes of its effects. Artists also do more than imagine things into existence, argues Dutch photographer Barbara Visser, "the artist can also accomplish something else: bring together different forms of knowledge and insight like an orchestrator" (266). As a result, that which makes art unique makes its successes similarly difficult to capture and reproduce. Malevinsky's Algebraic Formula might result in an object called a play, but it is less likely to produce a play of critical or commercial significance through adherence to structural rules alone.

Knowledge construction is itself a dramaturgical concern related to reception and authority. Both science and theater depend on reception within and beyond their disciplinary fields for funding and social influence. Both navigate the complexity of communication on multiple levels: to fellow experts, students, and the wider public. For theater artists, positive audience or critical reception offers more paths to economic capital beyond governmental funding streams that remain minimal for artistic research and development (R&D).[8] In calls for increased governmental support, performing arts advocates cite scientific studies that employ a range of quantitative measures from the social and natural sciences to certify impact in terms beyond revenue and attendance.[9] Although relatively well supported with funds and infrastructure, scientists anticipate limited public consumption of their research due to their fields' specialized language and methods. As a result, educators recognize the need to translate or transform disciplinary-specific knowledge into products that can reach a broad audience with the goals of attracting a steady stream of students to train into professionals and drafting public advocates who will support the fields' public funding.

Whether funding considerations or the expansive array of information streams and technological platforms and instruments has led scientists to artists or artists to scientists, we are in a new era of collaborative storymaking and knowledge building. Recent surges in disinformation campaigns regarding climate change and public health, for example, illustrate the pressing need for better ways to articulate and understand complex conditions with the goal of collective action. What better field of work for dramaturgs in their roles as what scholar Michael Chemers calls "practical aesthetic philosophers" (11), bridging multiple disciplinary and interpretive divides between production and audience, script(writer) and production team, practice and theory? Now is a moment of invention and, as Lincoln Center Theater dramaturg Anne Cattaneo asserts, "The real job of all good dramaturgs is to extend and explore territory that the theater has not yet made its own" (14).

The SciArt of Dramaturgy

For scientists, the impulse to collaborate with artists for the purpose of educating said public has grown more attractive, but there are also collaborations where the final outcome is imagined, not realized.[10] Whether such collaborations include an identified dramaturg, the projects themselves call for a dramaturgical sensibility to support, contextualize, and assess their storytelling. In her introduction to the *Routledge Handbook of Dramaturgy*, Magda Romanska, traces etymological, historical, and social strains of dramaturgy as a "field, skill, and profession" that tends to coalesce around the process, theories, and practices of meaning making around a given experience or an experience as it unfolds for its participants/viewers (7). Dramaturg as cosmologist is the role invited by Elinor Fuchs in her essay, "EF's Visit to a Small Planet: Some Questions to Ask a Play":

> *The puzzles may hold the key.* Assume that the dramatic world is entirely conscious, determinate, limited. Give an account of that world that attempts to consider the role of every element in that world—visual, aural, temporal, tonal, figural. . . . Of course you

> can construct meaning in this world in many different ways. Construct it in the most inclusive way you can. There will still be more to see.
>
> (9)

So prompted, this book follows in the footsteps of Shepherd-Barr's thesis in her *Science on Stage* that the science plays that come closest to interdisciplinary integration "enact the idea that they engage" and "avoid the pitfall of sloppily appropriating precise scientific concepts for vague, general purposes" (6). She devotes her final chapter to these "alternative" science plays, taking up dramaturgy as the means by which scientific content becomes dramatic form, often signified by postdramatic story architecture and the prominence of a "director's theatre," where a script and its production emerge simultaneously through an extended rehearsal process (200). In Shepherd-Barr's analysis, science dramaturgy in such plays works like adaptation rather than literal translation: "Instead of taking the science in isolation and attempting to explain its meaning in lay terms, these works transform it into primarily visual and physical terms" (205). This book focuses on new work without extensive production histories, some created in conjunction with educational residencies and others housed in opt-in digital performance spaces throughout the internet. It offers a glimpse of the next generation of "alternative" science theater collaborations and the ways dramaturgical insight might facilitate the creation, reception, and analysis of such work.

Each chapter is organized around a small set of case studies that illuminate shared characteristics, stakes, contexts, and questions. Where do the interests of theater artists and scientists productively and problematically converge and diverge? What new forms of imagining, doing, and learning might be possible with closer collaborations? What do our histories and our current chaotic present mean for our futures? Many of the pieces described are concerned with and about history and authority. Many of the artists mentioned seek to solidify or dislodge various legacies of discovery and influence. This is a presentist study of a landscape dominated by U.S. educational, artistic, and economic structures and authorities as those are the ones in which I build work. The turn of the twenty-first century is a moment where interdisciplinary research arcs become particularly fertile due to growing technological praxis where technology becomes an expression of/tool for collaboration across science and theater.[11] The gaps and absences that readers will find in this book reflect circumstances in both fields where participation in experimental, interdisciplinary, resource-demanding projects is constrained by inequities, many based on racial and socioeconomic privilege.

A Map of the World

Chapter 1 focuses on the **dramaturgy of biography**, an emphasis on science history and scientific expertise that shapes the form, content, and patterns of development and production that characterize twenty-first-century commercial science theater in the United States. The chapter tenders an abbreviated history of the Alfred P. Sloan Foundation's new play commissions and its broader goals to raise public awareness about science and scientists with scientist-centered stories promoting the social benefits of scientific research and discovery. The chapter also includes a discussion of new iterations of Carl Djerassi's "science-in-theatre" dramaturgy found in the University of Chicago's S.T.A.G.E. Collaboratory and in *BrainWorks*, a project among two neuroscientists and a playwright. These evolutions of a dramaturgy of biography tend to reinscribe the authority of the scientist to explain the world and disappear in the hand of the playwright, reflecting an intriguing portability of dramaturgical practice to scientific domains, but at what cost to theater's precarious institutional and social positions? The chapter closes with an analysis of Lauren Gunderson's corpus. A playwright who has amassed a healthy bibliography of new science plays largely outside of Sloan funding and without much attention from academics, Gunderson shares Sloan's mission to promote the social benefits of science and centers her work on historical women whose research contributions were minimized by institutional inequities. She also operates from the position that theater lends science credibility (instead of vice versa) because theater embraces rather than constrains creativity.

Chapter 2 focuses on a **dramaturgy of interdependence**, the first of two that explore environmental science–informed theater. The EMOS (Earth Matters on Stage) Festival, founded in 2004, has constructed its own pipeline of plays/performances and brought together self-defined climate playwrights and ecodramaturgs like its founders Theresa May (Theater in the Wild; University of Oregon) and Chantal Bilodeau (*The Artic Cycle*) with academics such as Una Chadhuri (New York University) and Wendy Arons (Carnegie Mellon University) to collaborate on scholarly volumes and conferences. May's notion of "ecodramaturgy" and her invocation of theater as civic engine echoes similar arguments of artist and educator Paul Brown

(University of New South Wales), who offers a perspective about the roles of science and theater in world building based on his training as a scientist and a theater artist. The chapter locates this dramaturgy of interdependence in a range of stylistically innovative and unpublished work focused on temporality and mutual dependence between humans and the environment: Sheila Callaghan's *(Not) Water*, a play that was supposed to be about Hurricane Katrina until Hurricane Sandy came to New York; *The Great Immensity* by Steve Cosson and Michael Friedman, possibly best known not for its continuing innovation of documentary/investigatory dramaturgy but for its $700,000 National Science Foundation (NSF) grant; and Fly Jamerson's *Frozen Fluid*, which weaves together a landscape of catastrophic change in the arctic with a scientific expert's nonbinary identity and their colleagues' reception of that fluidity. These examples demonstrate how sensory immersion and communal experience are key to making climate science meaningful not only because it is a site of epistemological contestation but also because an ecological point of view should include the human as one of many organisms in relationship with their environments. As such, individual and systemic points of intervention toward a nonextractive existence necessitate a radical shift away from human-centered conflicts and individual corrective actions.

Chapter 3 focuses on science theater that centers a **dramaturgy of participation**, exploring artists' and scientists' turn to noncredentialed collaborators. The disparity of institutional support (time, funding, resources) within systems of global capitalism has produced innovative collaborations between everyday individuals and researchers. The Citizen Science movement represents a strategy to engage the broader public in practices of the scientific method and scientific thinking. Likewise, participatory or community-based work has always been part of the arts landscape in the United States, and increasingly, artists and citizens have built a range of embodied activities and events, which have been models for academic coursework, service-learning programs, and community theater programming. The chapter takes up performance projects that embrace such possibilities found in everyday expertise such Leah Fondakowski's *SPILL* and the work of PearlDamour (particularly *Ocean Filibuster*) which mediate environmental disaster and how communities recover or endure. I return briefly to *The Great Immensity* and the critiques of its NSF funding to frame my own work on a new play, *Rollover*, written by a coastal geologist at the University of North Carolina at Chapel Hill. The complicated notion of "impact" assessment across scientific and artistic fields sets new work development processes against a larger backdrop of federal budgets and summons questions about the fragile partnerships complicated by differing expectations regarding outcomes. Can interdisciplinary projects be simultaneously scientifically and artistically credible since both fields assess effectivity with widely different scales of value and success? What are the risks and potential in compromise? Do the methodologically complex approaches offered by citizen scientist protocols and participatory research-based development of theatrical projects provide collaborators new modes of dramaturgy that can bridge disciplinary values and outcomes?

Chapter 4 turns to technology as art, science, and tool and the artists whose work employs a **dramaturgy of precarity** in its development, forms, and assessment properties. Starting with research found in the journal *Leonardo* "on the use of contemporary science and technology in the arts and, increasingly, the application and influence of the arts and humanities on science and technology" (www.leonardo.info/leonardo), the chapter examines the last decade of "SciArt"-applied interdisciplinary and *intra*disciplinary ideas and practices, often found in institutionally anchored R&D spaces with some freedom to risk ideas, imagination, and critique of systems. After a brief review of artists who find ways to embed work within existing scientific research labs or create artistic lab research spaces to coinvestigate phenomena facilitated by technology, the chapter takes a deeper dive into the work of "rhythm scientist" DJ Spooky (a.k.a. Paul D. Miller) whose partnerships help foment strains of experimental performance art, where scientific content becomes artistic form and digital technology a cultural aesthetic. The chapter closes with the pandemic-born theater company Theater in Quarantine, where a tiny closet in Brooklyn has become an entire world of grounded physical theater rendered in all dimensions through the praxis of immersive and remote performance, articulating new vocabularies and values of digitally informed theater.

The final chapter examines the **dramaturgy of care** at work in medical science spaces, focusing on collaborations between artists and medical institutions to train and educate undergraduate students, medical students, and other health personnel. In response to negative representations of patient-provider communication and necessitated by healthcare professionals' desire to reflect and respond to their own institutional experiences, practitioners of narrative medicine focus on embodied reading and expressive writing practices to transform clinical encounters. That disciplinary field remains rooted in literature and poetry but invites possibilities for theater/performance as modes of research to illuminate systemic bias, medicine's eugenic impulse toward particular mental/physical standards of the normal, and to draft creative, collaborative strategies of resistance to current systems of healthcare research, education, and practice. To that end, the chapter explores the innovations of two scholar/artists – Marina Tsaplina (Embodiment and Puppetry) and Anne Basting (Creative Care) – whose research methodologies might shift medical students and professionals away from empathy as outcome and more toward creativity as a critical analytic to employ in the pursuit of health equity.

Three Possibilities of Two Cultures Collaboration

The array of people and projects chronicled in this book are offered for those in search of models, modes, and means to dismantle institutional and intellectual divides that place artists and scientists in separate and unequal spheres. Using dramaturgy as a lens into and an analytic tool for collaborative projects offers three tantalizing possibilities for collaboration across the two cultures. First, dramaturgy in practice is part catalyst, part experimentation, part lab report and, as such, offers a range of tools already at work in scientific thinking. Second, employing dramaturgy's praxis, each field's experts might find strategies to reckon with the social world and the fundamental human costs of representation and innovation. Finally, to forge new forms that *enact* versus *translate* phenomena requires scientists to be open to artistic experimentation in multiple domains of representation (such as character, temporality, scale, motion, and more). Dramaturgs who can consider not just questions of form but also of "how the world is constituted, encountered, experience, imagined or known" can help science-informed collaborations reach audiences where they are while also nudging those same audiences toward complexities of thought and feeling needed to meet the challenges of the future (Wilson and Van Ruiten 24). Malevinsky argued that "Atmosphere – mood-color – never have, and never will, constitute drama" (326). The range of theater performance, even at his historical moment, proves this statement false; however, he was right to be concerned about how audiences might engage, let alone understand, forms that challenge or confound their expectations.[12] The artist and scientist should not constrain their imaginations and experiences into fixed models and modes chasing audience approval but should work together to contextualize current events/information so that audiences may improve their capacities to meet complicated, radical, even confusing experiences because these are our current reality, probable future, as well as representative of our history in all its fullness.

Notes

1 His emphasis.
2 See Litman pages 34–41 for a discussion of Mavelinsky's legal successes and failures.
3 See Schechter for a brief lineage of Lessing's influence.
4 I use this punctuation around this phrase throughout the text to indicate its invocation beyond Snow's original lecture.
5 See, for example, *Performance, Medicine and the Human* (Bloomsbury, 2020); *Performance and the Medical Body* (Bloomsbury Methuen, 2016); *Anatomy Live: Performance and the Operating Theatre* (Amsterdam University Press, 2008); *Staging Stigma: A Critical Examination of the American Freak Show* (Palgrave Macmillan, 2008).
6 Science advisers are regularly employed to provide input for storyworlds dependent on real or facsimile scientific theories and practices; however, dramaturgical function takes primacy over adherence to reality.
7 See Mejias et al. for a discussion of the STEM to STEAM transition in U.S. education policy, curricular funding, and continuing disciplinary tensions embedded in these interdisciplinary endeavors.
8 The Department of Defense's Congressionally Directed Medical Research Programs fiscal year 2021 funding for R&D was $274.9 million (https://cdmrp.army.mil/about/fundinghistory), double the budget for the entirety of National Endowment for the Arts (NEA) funding for that year ($167.5 million), a figure that is the same as it was for the NEA in 2010.
9 See the *Art's for Life*'s Sake report from the American Academy of Arts and Sciences for examples of scientific studies to support arguments for government funding of the arts.
10 See Mejias et al., pages 219–220 and 223–224 for examples.
11 See, for example, *Practicing Art/Science: Experiments in an Emerging Field* (Routledge, 2019) and *Dialogues between Artistic Research and Science and Technology Studies* (Routledge, 2020).
12 See Davies for an extended analysis of the emotional labor required of curiosity, a desired audience outcome of public science festivals where arts products and practices are used to create engagements.

References

American Academy of Arts and Sciences. *Art for Life's Sake: The Case for Arts Education*. 2021. www.amacad.org/project/commission-arts.

Case, Sue-Ellen. *Performing Science and the Virtual*. Routledge, 2007.

Cattaneo, Anne. "Dramaturgy: An Overview." *Dramaturgy in American Theatre: A Source Book*, edited by Susan Jonas, Geoffrey S. Proehl, and Michael Lupu. Harcourt Brace, 1997, pp. 3–13.

Chemers, Michael M. *Ghost Light: An Introductory Handbook for Dramaturgy*. Southern Illinois University Press, 2010.

Davies, Sarah R. "Science Communication as Emotion Work: Negotiating Curiosity and Wonder at a Science Festival." *Science as Culture*, vol. 28, no. 4, 2019, pp. 538–561. doi:10.1080/09505431.2019.1597035.

Fuchs, Elinor. "EF's Visit to a Small Planet: Some Questions to Ask a Play." *Theater*, vol. 34, no. 2, 2004, pp. 5–9.

Kuhn, Thomas S. *The Structure of Scientific Revolutions.* University of Chicago Press, 1962.

Latour, Bruno. *Science in Action: How to Follow Scientists and Engineers Through Society.* Harvard University Press, 1987.

Litman, Jessica. "Silent Similarity." *Chicago-Kent Journal of Intellectual Property*, vol. 14, no. 1, 2014, pp. 11–47. *HeinOnline.* heinonline.org/HOL/P?h=hein.journals/ jointpro14&i=11.

Malevinsky, Moses L. *The Science of Playwriting*. Brentano's, 1925.

Mejias, Sam, et al. "The Trouble with STEAM and Why We Use It Anyway." *Science Education*, vol. 105, 2021, pp. 209–231. doi:10.1002/sce.21605.

Oreskes, Naomi. "Why Should We Believe in Science?" *TED Radio Hour*, "Spirit of Inquiry." NPR. 24 Feb. 2017. npr.org/2017/02/24/516709308/naomi-oreskes-why-should-we-believe-in-science.

Proehl, Geoffrey S. "The Images Before Us: Metaphors for the Role of the Dramaturg in American Theater." *Dramaturgy in American Theatre: A Source Book*, edited by Susan Jonas, Geoffrey S. Proehl, and Michael Lupu. Harcourt Brace, 1997, pp. 124–136.

Reproducibility and Replicability in Science. The National Academies of Sciences, Engineering, and Medicine, 2019. doi:10.17226/25303.

Romanska, Magda, editor. *The Routledge Companion to Dramaturgy.* Routledge, 2015.

Schechter, Joel. "In the Beginning There Was Lessing … Then Brecht, Muller, and Other Dramaturgs." *Dramaturgy in American Theatre: A Source Book*, edited by Susan Jonas, Geoffrey S. Proehl, and Michael Lupu. Harcourt Brace, 1997, pp. 16–24.

Shepherd-Barr, Kirsten, editor. *The Cambridge Companion to Theatre and Science.* Cambridge University Press, 2020.

Shepherd-Barr, Kirsten, editor. *Science on Stage: From Doctor Faustus to Copenhagen*. Princeton University Press, 2006.

Snow, C.P. *The Two Cultures and the Scientific Revolution*. Cambridge University Press, 1961.

Visser, Barbara. "A Blind Man Sometimes Hits the Crow." *See It Again, Say It Again: The Artist as Researcher*, edited by Janneke Wesseling. Valiz, 2011, pp. 255–266.

Wilson, Mick, and Schelte Van Ruiten, editors. *SHARE Handbook for Artistic Research Education*. ELIA, 2013.

1 Dramaturgy of Biography

Theater as Science's Public Relations Unit

Founder of the S.T.A.G.E. Collaboratory, Nancy Kawalek opens her 2016 TEDx Talk with this provocation: "If science illuminates the way the world works and theater illuminates the way people work, aren't they a perfect match?" Her question encapsulates the impetus behind one of the longest running science play development engines in the United States: the Alfred P. Sloan Foundation, a philanthropic organization with an almost 90-year history funding original research and education in STEM fields. Sloan's Public Understanding of Science, Technology & Economics program overseen by Doron Weber since its inception at the turn of the twenty-first century began with commissions hosted by off-Broadway and Broadway institutions – Ensemble Studio Theatre (EST) and Manhattan Theatre Club (MTC). In the past two decades, its commissioning and awards influence has expanded to include a rotating network of regional theaters, the audio theater production company L.A. Theatre Works (LATW), and London's National Theatre.

In her book *Science: Dramatic. Science Plays in American and Great Britain 1990–2007*, Eva-Sabine Zehelein notes how the "invisible hand of the marketplace" influenced the growth of science plays on commercial stages since the late 1990s. She mentions Sloan in passing, as part of "councils and foundations" who function as "P.R.-agents" for science, a field where everyday research work is often invisible to the public, but the field's catastrophic, controversial, or scandalous news can have an outsized influence on public perceptions (5). Zehelein argues entities like Sloan with missions to improve the public's understanding about science and scientists demonstrate "gatekeep[ing]" at work in such arts funding: "selections have an agenda-setting function and can constitute a decisive factor for a play's commercial success, or

DOI: 10.4324/9781003150848-2

at least its public perception" (5). Sloan funds scientific research directly and supports film, theater, and fiction projects that valorize the scientific process and profession, emulating chemist-playwright Carl Djerassi's notion of "science-in-theater." A vocal critic of popular culture representations of science as well as theater scholarship about science plays, Djerassi held specific standards for both what he defined as science and its appearance in creative products (Grünzweig). Zehelein summarizes Djerassi's own "science-in-theater" plays as presenting a world where "at the core of both theme and plot, the science being described is 'real,' both science and scientists, are realistically depicted and, finally, the didactic element of explaining a scientific context features prominently" ("Staging It" 4–5). As he evolved his dual expertise, Djerassi evolved his scripts to include less lecture-style presentational elements of research (such as his own work in human reproduction) and more of "the culture and behavior of science [and scientists]," a kind of "tribe" to which he belonged and whose inner-workings are often not experienced or are misunderstood by the general public (Barnett). He turned his dramatic attentions to the private lives of historical scientists and the dynamics of professional negotiations – disciplinary, authorial, and institutional – that shape what and about whom we learn from the history of science. Djerassi staked out particular territories in the representation of science for a broad public and advocated using information that is vetted and verifiable that can ease an audience's experience of radical paradigm shifts, promoting clarity over confusion, coalition over fragmentation.

The **dramaturgy of biography** at work in this so-influenced strain of science theater includes scientist-centered stories that dramatize protagonists' networks of personal and professional relationships, their intellectual drives and passions, highlighting key moments of discovery and the social benefits of scientific research. With that in mind, this chapter traces the origins, influence, and limits of Sloan's commissioning engine and identifies two new iterations of "science-in-theater" projects: Kawalek's S.T.A.G.E. Collaboratory and the BrainWorks series, composed by a playwright working with neuroscientists. These represent a different "two cultures" tension at work—namely, between the commercial and the educational—and illustrate some enduring promises and pitfalls when theater is employed as a dramaturgical "fixer" to promote the humanity of scientists and science. Such a dynamic also exists in the robust catalog of science plays by Lauren Gunderson whose work has achieved commercial success largely outside the influence of Sloan and without much academic analysis. The chapter concludes by illustrating the ways in which

Gunderson's focus on underrepresented women of science history emphasizes biography as a key dramaturgical value of commercial, U.S. science theater.

EST to *Copenhagen* Time

The Sloan Foundation began its foray into theater production in 1997 with funding support for Arthur Giron's *Flight* about the childhoods of Orville and Wilbur Wright. Doron Weber, at the time Sloan's relatively new head of their Public Understanding program, was impressed by Giron's "very human approach to the subject." In a 2001 profile of science theater for the *New York Times*, Weber told reporter Robert Meyers that at Sloan, "part of my goal is to humanize scientists. We tend to have this gap, an inability to see scientists as ordinary people." The next year, Sloan formalized a relationship with EST where Giron was a founding member through a $504,000 "theatrical R&D" grant and the creation of the First Light Festival named for the idea in astronomy of the first, often unrefined, view of an astronomical body through a telescope (Powell 86). In 1999, EST announced ten new Sloan commissions and its support of a full production of *Tesla's Letters* by Jeffery Stanley. By the time EST hosted its second First Light Festival, headlines about a new "wave" of science plays and the Sloan Foundation's role in their creation started to appear in mainstream and science news outlets.

Separate from these developments, *Copenhagen* premiered in 1998 at Britain's National Theatre to great critical and audience acclaim. Michael Frayn was inspired by a meeting in 1941 Nazi-occupied Denmark between nuclear scientists Werner Heisenberg and Niels Bohr and "the philosophical implications of quantum mechanics, . . . between the uncertainty of people's motivations and the uncertainty in the behavior of physical objects" (Meyers). Although Sloan gave no funding to *Copenhagen*'s writing, Frayn was an invited speaker at EST's second First Light Festival in the spring of 2000. They also provided funding for a daylong symposium, "Creating *Copenhagen*," to coincide with *Copenhagen*'s arrival on Broadway. Brian Schwartz, a professor of physics at Brooklyn College, crafted the symposium and built on its success to create a "Science & the Arts" series at the new Graduate Center at CUNY, including a 2003 *Staging Science* course he cotaught with theater historian Marvin Carlson. Schwartz received a 2005 NSF grant of $680,000 for his "Science as Performance: A Proactive Strategy to Communicate and Educate through Theater, Music and Dance" proposal under the "Integrative Activities in

Physics" category. With this funding, he produced 120 events of "science to the general public via the performing arts – theater, music, dance, the literary and visual arts, magic and scientific demonstrations" over 13 years (Schwartz 279, 281). These events continued a focus on esteemed historical figures (such as Benjamin Franklin, Charles Darwin) along with presenting new work by choreographers Liz Lerman and Elizabeth Streb, public lecture/demonstrations about architecture, origami, geometry, and string theory, as well as supplemental, educational programming around large theatrical events, such as the 2008 performances of Peter Sellars's and John Adams's *Doctor Atomic* at the Metropolitan Opera.

MTC and *Proof* Positive

Back in New York, MTC discovered its own science play success with David Auburn's *Proof*. The story of a young mathematics researcher who moves home to care for her dying, mathematician father, *Proof* began its off-Broadway run mere weeks before *Copenhagen*'s Tony win in May 2000 and moved to Broadway's Walter Kerr theater in October. While it was not the commissioning force behind *Proof* 's development either, Sloan provided key funding for outreach around *Proof*'s production in the form of symposia contextualizing issues regarding women in math and explaining the various mathematical theories its characters engaged in their research (Denzell). *Copenhagen* and *Proof* overlapped their Broadway runs for about four months. Auburn won the 2001 Pulitzer Prize for drama, and the production took home the Tony for Best Play. Like *Copenhagen, Proof* toured the country for eight months, but there was no organized science symposium effort around it (Henerson). Instead, a second science play commissioning partnership was born between Sloan and MTC. In 2001, Sloan announced the MTC partnership and renewed its collaboration with EST for another three-year cycle (Horwitz).

By the time the *New York Times* published a 2003 feature "Lab Coat Chic: The Arts Embrace Science" to discuss the "recent spate of films and plays" about science and scientists and to publicize Sloan's first Sundance Film Festival awards (Overbye), EST and Sloan had announced the National Partnership for New Plays (NP≈), supporting regional theaters "who wish to sponsor a local project focused on science and technology, either by commissioning a new script or developing an existent piece" (Rabinowitz). In 2003, those theaters were Actor's Theatre of Louisville, Cleveland Play House, Minneapolis's the Guthrie Theater, the Magic Theatre (San Francisco), and Victory

Gardens Theatre (Chicago). EST founder, Curt Dempster, is quoted in a 2003 interview with the *Boston Globe* that in five years his theater had "awarded 90 artists, composers, choreographers, and theater companies more than $150,000 to develop new works" through its Sloan program (Foster). That same year, Sloan renewed the collaboration with $1 million in funding.

By 2007, a new circuit emerged to build a wider audience for Sloan-commissioned and other well-known science plays that had a New York run or West Coast production. Sloan granted L.A. Theater Works (LATW) $253,000 to record four previously commissioned plays and start new monthly series called *Relativity.* Susan Loewenberg, LATW's founder and producing director, described the initiative as underwriting free theater for the public good:

> A new play will be featured every month and each play will stay up for three months.... Whenever possible, plays in The Relativity Series will be scheduled to coincide with anniversaries of scientific discovery and scientists' lives, and programming will also be thematically coordinated with other existing public radio programming such as Ira Flatow's NPR program *Science Friday.*
>
> (Deni)

Since much of this early-twenty-first-century science play canon dramatizes the lives of historical figures, their discoveries, and general positivist narratives, it seems logical that *Relativity* draws from Sloan commissions for the majority of its audio catalog. As of 2021, it houses a roster of 37 recordings free to listen via SoundCloud, including recent plays such as Charly Evon Simpson's *Behind the Sheet* (2019). Interviews with scientific or historical experts provide contextual lectures or conversations for the Sloan commissions (latw.org/relativity-series).

It is difficult to determine the size of individual commissions from news stories and press releases. By 2019, EST's Sloan partnership grant had grown to $1.92 million taking the commissions program through 2022. When *American Theatre* announced the MTC/Sloan 2020 commissions for six writers, the editors quoted MTC's current director of play development, Scott Kaplan, saying there had been 94 commissions in the 19 years of the partnership. These funds supported the work of many artists; however, a robustly funded path from commission to development to production seems more elusive. If the end game is a broader cultural shift in how science and scientists are perceived but scripts remain only at the commission versus production phase, what alternative paths are possible for science theater development?

Collaboratory Stories

Around the time Sloan branched out into audio recording of plays, Nancy Kawalek founded S.T.A.G.E. – *S*cientists, *T*echnologists and *A*rtists *G*enerating *E*xploration at the University of California, Santa Barbara. Her early efforts centered on hosting an international competition for the "best new play about science and technology," selecting five plays between 2006 and 2012 with two centered on figures from history: Anna Ziegler's *Photograph 51* (2008) about Watson and Crick collaborator Rosalind Franklin and Elyse Singer's *Frequency Hopping* (2007) about the lesser-known scientific achievements of Hollywood actress Hedy Lamarr. In her TEDx Talk, Kawalek notes that the majority of submissions sent to the S.T.A.G.E. competition held a rather negative view of science and technology. Plots often centered on grotesque experiments let loose on an unsuspecting public by unethical creators. The next most frequent entries were those that invoked a dramaturgy of biography: historical portraits of either well-known or unknown scientists we should know due to their critical contributions to key discoveries.

Even before Kawalek had assumed leadership of the Arts, Sciences and Technology research theme at the University of Chicago's Institute for Molecular Engineering (IME, now PME as it became the Pritzker School of Molecular Engineering in 2019), she had already started to shift the focus in S.T.A.G.E. from a script competition to a development engine for performances authored by its own roster of artistic collaborators inspired by and actively pursuing scientific research. The university was already a few years into its Arts, Science & Culture Initiative to encourage transdisciplinary research between graduate students in the arts and the sciences, funding their shared investigations over an academic year (Bauld). In her TED Talk, Kawalek discusses the influence of Canadian theater artist Robert Lepage and his Ex Machina company, who build from existing texts and new technologies, intertwining forms across dance, music, and theater. Such a multidisciplinary approach to creation seemed to reflect the way she heard scientists talk about "accidental discoveries" during experiments and the trail of investigation opened up by failures or by "blips" in data that confound one hypothesis but engender another. She decided her "collective laboratory" would make its own theater, the first in 2009 titled *The Brain Project*, which would become by the time of its full, public performance in 2017 *The Art of Questionable Provenance* (Institute for Molecular Engineering 17).[1]

As of 2021, there are multiple projects with a "coming soon" designation on the S.T.A.G.E. website. Some, like *Art of*, culminate in theatrical performances and others are bound for other mediums: animation, virtual reality, and interactive installations or exhibits. Although correlation between theater and laboratory has been the subject of some criticism,[2] S.T.A.G.E. frames its collaboratory's process as "directly inspired by the exploratory process of experimental science" (stage.pme.uchicago.edu/about/work_process). Theater artists might also recognize elements of this approach as similar to devised work. In her TEDx Talk, Kawalek describes how the research group starts brainstorming the "emotional essence, i.e., metaphors for the science," and out of these, they build a "personal parallel" to that science. These metaphors become the basis for collaborators to compile resources, which can be "anything – a research paper … a newspaper article, a film clip, a photograph, a personal anecdote." The team of scientific researchers, performers, designers, and technicians work with these materials simultaneously in shared space because "the sum is greater than any of its elements." Working in the same room with materials gathered from disciplinary specialties while explaining information *across* those specialties produces the "blurred boundary" where Kawalek argues both fields can "wonder" and ruminate on that "exquisite moment when the unexpected presents itself."

My discussion of S.T.A.G.E. centers on *Art of* because it had a relatively lengthy gestation period for any new play – eight years. Such a long development process, however, may not be unusual for S.T.A.G.E. Also, professional playwrights play a relatively minor role in the work's creation. The 14-person production team mentioned in *Art of* promotional materials online includes five designers, five scientists, and four actors, one of whom has experience as a playwright. In the 2017 year-end report for IME, the project is described as the result of "more than twenty scientists and artists, including actors, writers, dramaturgs, and designers" who "wove the complex story" starting with "improvisation" to find how the "scientific analysis of artwork" connected with "the science of human thought" (Institute for Molecular Engineering 16). Kawalek describes to her TEDx audience how each "improvisation is treated like an experiment. We're constantly weighing and examining what the experiments tell us."[3] In *Art of*, S.T.A.G.E. employs the art museum as a backdrop for a scientific investigation into the mysteries of human behavior. Artist and scientist characters are brought together under an unusual circumstance to detect, each with their own expertise, a "mystery" that surrounds a particular piece of art and its creation. They employ visual technologies in their investigation. A bank of screens dominates the performance space, and visualizations illustrate scientific concepts, expose that which is beneath the body's surface and under layers of paint and pixels, and expand the theatrical universe with photorealistic representations of other spaces and places and the technologies we use to navigate them (from digital maps to apps to microscopy). Kawalek cites this integration as the kind of experimentation that S.T.A.G.E.'s theatrical work pursues. It can test and reflect machines' digital processing power but also dramatize technology's legacy of influences on visual perception and, by extension, on characters' conception of self and reality.

Art of offers a hybrid dramatic form between science lecture/demonstration, science fiction's imagined worlds, and postdramatic experience as story. The lack of published scripts or academic analysis on the theatrical contributions of S.T.A.G.E., however, indicates the benefits of the lab's generative research might remain enclosed in a circle of scientists and engineers instead of available to theater artists. In 2020, S.T.A.G.E. launched a docuseries pilot, *Curiosity: The Making of a Scientist*. The show follows an individual University of Chicago scientist through their professional and personal experiences, intertwining fields and feelings to inspire a viewer with either greater respect for the journey or a desire to pursue that path themselves. Perhaps this step away from the theater stage reflects a desire on the part of S.T.A.G.E. collaborators for their materials to reach a wider audience as an educational tool. The product, however, still reflects core dimensions of the dramaturgy of biography: a protagonist who dreams of scientific discovery accomplished through tenacity, ingenuity, and dedication, conveying the scope and aspirations of their research through by dynamic storytelling elements that try to dramatize the world as it exists and the world that science (and story) makes possible.

The Stage of the Mind

Playwright John Walch summarizes *BrainWorks* as "a one-act play mashed up with a TED Talk" (Liwag). The head of the University of Arkansas, Fayetteville's MFA in playwriting program, Walch first joined the project when neurosurgeons Eric Leuthardt and Albert Kim partnered with New Dramatists playwrights in 2011 to craft short plays from their patient files. Leuthardt and Kim, colleagues at the Washington School of Medicine in St. Louis and the Barnes-Jewish Hospital had collaborated on a speaker's series, a podcast, and various TED Talks. In a July 9, 2019 interview with St. Louis Public Radio to promote a "live, on-stage" iteration of *BrainWorks*,[4] the physicians discussed the relatively staid nature of other forms and their embrace of theater as a matter of empathy, a need to stimulate the emotions in order to engage their audiences and discuss scientific ideas. Almost two decades after Doron Weber stated his mission for Sloan's theater commissions as "humanizing scientists," these neurosurgeons reiterated the usefulness of theater to produce feelings which in turn produce knowledge or, at least, the investment in learning: "The more you can get people imagining through things like the arts the better off we are in the future" (Ahl).

The four short plays that comprise *BrainWorks* present a familiar science play storyline, particularly for works about medicine: unknown issues afflict a character and a dedicated scientist deciphers the clues, offers a diagnosis, and the character engages that diagnosis with outcomes that are positive, if not wholly restorative. *BrainWorks*' stories are linked together through the characters' experiences of neurological conditions and the support they receive from physicians and caregivers. Leuthardt and Kim reinforce the veracity of medical research, as they traverse the stage in their everyday roles as teachers and surgeons, narrating diagnostic details, even appearing as themselves in scenes. And while presented as a unique approach, the structure reflects Djerassi's "science-in-theater" features: "real science with real scientists" and "using the theatre for scientific enlightenment" (*An Immaculate Misconception x*). For his part, Walch contributed both a specific script, *Double Windsor*, about the loss of limb use after a stroke, while also serving as story editor for the four pieces that were crafted into an evening of performance filmed for television broadcast. He is largely absent by name from the scientists' publicity, but the University of Arkansas's press office resurrects his role in the process while also deferring to the expertise of Leuthardt and Kim: "The project began with the doctors, and their desire to share their research and what excites them about the incredible progress being made in their areas of research, and so they are the center of the evening" (Liwag). Similarly, in *BrainWorks*' public broadcasting promotional materials and interviews with the doctors and their teaching hospital employer, theater artists are cast as facilitators of the scientists' expertise, bringing it into accord with audience expectations. The surgeons talk in general terms about artists who help them shape dialogue and emotion, but as neurologists, they claim unique insight into cognition and theories of reception and emotion. They describe the theater as a final frontier laboratory, one of key importance because it is where audiences exist and where critical impressions of the modes, mechanics, and mentality of science and scientists are forged.

In an intriguing callback to 19th-century public science lectures, the proliferation of forums like the TED Talk and podcasts seem to have expanded scientists' confidence in their ability to communicate their research. For Leuthardt and Kim, however, even charisma, expertise, and compelling narratives from their clinical practice were insufficient to produce the kind of accessible, relatable experiences that would produce "more informed patients" (Ahl). For this, they turned to the empathy promised by the theater via *BrainWorks*, asserting themselves as helpful narrators in and around patient stories. Such belief in empathy to drive individual knowledge and social change supports the power of theater as a collaborative partner to science. The question emerges, however, as to what happens to theater artists with interests in creating work on scientific fields and topics without the aid of an invested scientist or scientific research institution? Lauren Gunderson's work offers some clues to a new era of commercial appeal of science plays engaging a dramaturgy of biography that centers women.

Officiating the Marriage of Science and Theater

An artist who enjoys the title of America's most produced living playwright (2017–19), Lauren Gunderson sits at the head of the class of U.S. science playwriting. Her work has been produced with commercial success largely outside the kickstart of Sloan, and she enjoys fruitful, ongoing relationships with various regional theaters as well as audiobook giant Audible. The reach of *The Catastrophist* (2021) and *The Half-Life of Marie Curie* (2020) via streaming and digital technologies will likely continue to fuel her success (Marks). Gunderson expresses optimism for the essential value of science and touts its partnership with theater as an opportunity for the fields to enhance each other. Her efforts to humanize, diversify, and ground science in theatrical storytelling that "lift[s] up [STEM] subjects for the respect that they deserve" (Handlesman and Smith), elevates theater's reputation as well. For such a prolific and commercially successful playwright, there is a surprising lack of scholarship about her work. There have been profiles, interviews, podcasts, and reviews starting in 2004 after her senior year at Atlanta's Emory University when she enjoyed two professional productions of plays she wrote as a student (Li). Gunderson contributes op-eds to news outlets focused on the arts, the sciences, and politics and is the only professional theater artist on the Aspen Institute's Science and Society Advisory Council, an entity she was instrumental in creating. To date, however, her work has not yet been the subject of significant academic analysis.

Seyedeh Anahit Kazzazi mentions Gunderson in his 2017 article, "The Anatomy of the Science Play," where he organizes an array of British and American science theater plays written after 1990 into a taxonomy based on the type of role science plays in the story: supporting character, main character, or director. In his examples, a writer's hand guides the script's creation and the "science as director" role reflects how scientific theories and experiments influence a science play's staging (338). Kazzazi does not include dramaturg in his list of roles for science to play, nor do Gunderson's plays figure significantly in his article. Revising his construct slightly, I argue *science as dramaturg* more aptly describes its function in Gunderson's science plays, especially the way creativity motivates her central characters' scientific intelligence and innovation, both needed to press the boundaries of the unknown and to understand and appreciate what one discovers there. What follows is an analysis of plays that populate two of the three veins by which Gunderson characterizes her playwriting: first, "plays … with a kind of feminist understanding or reinvestigation of history and science; … and second, outliers [plays that resist or put a twist on] straight naturalism." Within her "STEM-centric" (Weinert-Kendt) plays, there are three constants that harken to a dramaturgy of biography: (1) the integration of mechanics of scientific inquiry within the play's form, (2) the centrality of love and devotion on the part of her women protagonists, which often clashes with their success in a scientific field, and (3) the force of physical change (specifically, illness) to upend the trajectory of her protagonists' scientific research, discovery, and achievement.

Form = Function

Gunderson credits an undergraduate physics professor who allowed her to write a play instead of a term paper for her drive to investigate broad scientific fields – astronomy, chemistry, coding, mathematics, physics (most frequently), and virology (most recently) – through playwriting ("Eureka Stories"). Her central goal is the clear, compelling communication of basic scientific principles and disciplinary histories, while imparting lessons about what it means to be human. When queried for specifics of her science background, Gunderson admits she was always a writer in search of subject matter worthy of her passion for artistic creation. With the support of key teachers, she found that subject matter in science ("Eureka Stories"). For Gunderson, theater's multisensory form offers her the opportunity to construct "complex journey[s] towards new coherence," where scientist protagonists try and fail and fail again, but by the end, they and the audience arrive at a place where "we've learned something" (Wallace and Campbell). In a 2011 op-ed for the *Wall Street Journal*, she writes,

> Plays are designed to be sensory experiences as much as literary ones. They are words crafted for delivery by live bodies in a shared physical space and time. Because the audience is in the same room with the story, plays are uniquely visceral.
> ("The Ending of the Play's the Thing")

This primacy of feeling helps pave the way for what Gunderson calls in that same editorial the "inevitable surprise" of an ending, something you suspect might happen but are still charmed or horrified when it does. If one thinks of plays as experiments,[5] this idea of "inevitable surprise" is one that connects the theatrical with the scientific, a highly controlled investigation of known boundaries, with the hope that one might glimpse something or some path toward something new and as yet undefined.

Gunderson's approach reflects what Liliane Campos identifies as science as a "structuring schemata" (303). Campos cites Nick Payne's *Constellations* and Complicite's *A Disappearing Number* as examples of such an approach, plays that feature "postdramatic fragmentation, replacing linear, causal plots by other narrative logics" from the "less rational" corners of scientific thinking (304). Gunderson's work is firmly textual and invested in processual rising action toward a reveal or twist; however, she also employs elements of postdramatic dramaturgy such as simultaneity, the unfolding of action in reverse, and repeated patterns in imagery, language, and sound. In Gunderson's corpus, one can find dimensions of Campos's notion of how science plays employ scientific language and terminology as "both epistemological and poetic, because they belong to scientific models but function as metaphors" (298).

Gunderson focuses on "finding great moments of change" in the lives of her scientist characters and investigating what prompted or resulted from that change. Frequently, those moments revolve around love, marriage, birth, or death as much as they do around discovery, challenge, failure, or acclaim. As the titular character asserts in *Emilie:*

La Marquise du Châtelet Defends Her Life Tonight, "*Lives aren't equations…* . They are variables *inside* them/the governing equations are universal,/but a life lived fully can still change the universe" (71). While many postdramatic science plays take a critical view of positivism, Gunderson is its cheerleader. In science, particularly science history and women in science history, there are "rich characters, [who] want something, and they go through something big" and these elements permeate Gunderson's plays ("Eureka Stories"). Science, she argues, is "this collection of change-making ideas over and over again" with "deep and thrilling stories [about] the course of scientific progress" (Wallace and Campbell).[6] Perhaps this more generous view of progress could be attributed to Gunderson's investment in the stories of forgotten, overlooked, or unknown women of science. To undercut a grand narrative of scientific achievement before these hidden figures have been given their due would be counterproductive. Gunderson's characters often express doubt and worry about their authority, knowledge, and abilities, but because their discoveries have already been vetted by history, a contemporary audience can place their concerns in proper context, safe in the knowledge that their skill and imagination prove them worthy.

Gunderson's characters enact Snow's "two cultures" debate repeatedly, often asserting the superiority of science because its pursuit implies one can escape the frustration of human attachments. For example, Ada and her poet father debate the two when they meet in the afterlife of *Ada and the Engine*:

BYRON: Machines cannot better us, they've got no heart. Machines cannot love.

ADA: Good for them.

BYRON: You would really want that? To be heartless and cold?

ADA: Painless and unburdened, yes I rather think I would've preferred that.

BYRON: And this from a daughter of a Romantic.

ADA: From a daughter who trusted numbers more than people. Numbers do not lie, nor leave, nor die.

(68–69)

And as Nathan rails about his wife, the playwright, in *The Catastrophist*:

NATHAN: Theatre is *not* science. That I know. It's the opposite. She makes the ending whatever she wants it to be. I can't do that. In fact that would be scientific fraud. Is there theatrical fraud? Isn't that what theatre *is*? Very nice, well-lit fraud?

(6)

Similarly, Emilie accuses her lover, Voltaire:

EMILIE: For *once* just consider the idea that you *could* be mistaken, that you *could* be fallible in this *one* scenario, lonely as it may be in the immensity of your usual correctness. Science isn't theatre, you can't pick the ending because it sounds nice.

(38)

Theater, however, provides these characters chances for revelation and reversal. It cannot deny death in the material world, but it can replay, recast, recalibrate how one's life is lived over the span of a play. And unlike the scientific experiment that once set in motion typically runs its course and its results are evaluated as successful or unsuccessful, theater can change the rules under which a particular experiment is conducted as it happens. As the central character/historical figure of Gunderson's *Background* reminds us, "when studying the beginning [of the universe], you must work backwards to find it" (7).[7] In one of her most popular plays, *I And You*, this end as beginning structure provides the piece with a tantalizing twist that, once known, affects how one experiences, sees, or reads the play again.

Life and Love Catalyze Inquiry

Gunderson constructs worlds wherein we experience science embedded in the scientist's social context. For Gunderson, "effective science" within a play must be combined with "effective poetry to create something that is true both in the concrete and the abstract… . The best scientific characters do all the things that make us human, not just the things that make us brilliant" ("Science Plays Come of Age"). Given her investment in the public's impressions about science, it is surprising that Sloan has played such a minimal role in developing her plays, and yet it might offer one reason for this. Instead of artists serving science's purposes, capturing and conveying facts, in Gunderson's world it is scientific ideas that need artists' life-giving forces of play and creativity. Without art, there is no spark; without such spark, scientific ideas and their thinkers lack the communicative force to change the world. From her first full-length work, *Leap*, Gunderson has insisted that science's most inspired discoveries are not possible without creativity. In *Leap*, Maria and Brightman are teenaged muses who engage Newton (seen only by him) through the processes that produce some of his most fruitful postulations. They refer to having visited other transformational geniuses – Leonardo da Vinci, Galileo Galilei – but they sense that Newton is someone whose theories will change everything.

The young women carry a Book of Games and pick from it to stimulate his thinking. They also navigate a mix of romantic and filial love for the young scholar as he struggles with the isolation required by the plague, his family duties, and mathematical insights just outside his grasp. They debate just how much they can or should reveal to their charge,[8] and the scenes, while moving forward in linear time, also run simultaneously as one set of characters posits and another set of characters discovers:

BRIGHTMAN: [unseen by Isaac's manservant Lucas] Think of how many … shades of loving there are. Not even shades, completely different colors of love: maternal, fraternal, romantic, patriotic… . An entire spectrum … all contained in one *white* word.

LUCAS: (*reads from Isaac's notebook*) "White light being composed of every colour in the spectrum which can be separated through refraction devices … "

MARIA: Brightman …

BRIGHTMAN: Or unrequited love. The kind that sends a girl sliding on the *curve* of emotion. Up and down with each glance and hope of mutual attraction. The losing party trying to get so close but the closer one gets in the approach the more impossible it is to reach. Traveling further and further but never reaching, always *approaching the limit* of …

LUCAS: (*Reading*) "The limit of a function is the x value as it approaches but never *equals* zero … "

(75–76)

This scene demonstrates the motivation that emotions provide in the so-called objective world of science. Newton incorporates Brightman's sentiments into his laws of motion by translating scientific terms into layman's terms. Such clarity helps Gunderson's characters counter other stereotypical perceptions of scientific research and its practitioners: passionless and yet in possession of knowledge that can unlock the universe's secrets.

The fears and frustrations of possibility tie together human relationships (romantic, familial) and scientific inquiry in Gunderson's work, and her women characters experience greater success cracking scientific questions than breaking through social and cultural conventions. A meeting of the minds – Ada and Charles in *Ada and the Engine* – cannot bridge an age difference nor difference in class status. A battle of wills – Henrietta and Peter in *Silent Sky* – becomes a substitute for romance as familial duty and a single-minded focus on recognition causes him to come to the thought of partnership too soon and for her it comes too late. A collaboration – Emilie and Voltaire in *Emilie: La Marquise du Châtelet Defends Her Life Tonight* – becomes a competition and a realization for Emilie that in a heterosexual coupling, unconventional men will always be able to walk away from partnership with fewer consequences than unconventional women. Hindsight is Gunderson's dramaturgical assistant, allowing the playwright to draw on contemporary knowledge to vindicate radical assertions from these historical women of science: Ada's theories about "analytical engines," i.e., computers; Emilie's input on the formula for kinetic energy that paved the way for Einstein's E-mc^2; Henrietta's detections of patterns of pulsation became the basis for Hubble to calculate our galaxy's expanse and multiplicity. This hindsight introduces another commonality among these plays. Men, with the entire world at their disposal, tend to limit their vision and foment jealousies regarding credit and acclaim. Women, constrained by social and familial expectations, follow their impulses while also putting in diligent work to craft the capacity for visionary thinking.

The End as Beginning

Gunderson's women protagonists confront social and cultural challenges as they seek participation in and recognition from the world of science. Gunderson's men protagonists experience the physical effects of stress that accompanies the rejection, neglect, or misinterpretation of their scientific work. *The Catastrophist* helps vindicate the actions of the play's single character, virologist Nathan, from a charge that he mishandled a previous outbreak. Written in 2021 but set in 2016 when most Americans' understanding of pandemics was historical, the play's action takes place when Nathan undergoes surgery to clear a blocked artery, avoiding a "widowmaker" heart attack. Such an unexpected event also begins of one of her earliest plays, *Background*, about mathematician Ralph Alpher's overlooked contributions to astrophysics. For the women, there are physical effects too – each heroine tends to die in childbirth or from cancer – and we see them battle to stay connected to their work for as long as possible. From beyond the grave, these women assert their professional achievements are secondary to having freedom to think and learn for themselves. As Emilie notes, "And for the first time in my life I think that happiness may not be *having* all the answers... . It may be having time and space to wonder" (32). In a space between life and death, *Silent Sky's* Henrietta Leavitt discovers her calculations have been used by a (male) astronomer, Hubble, to support the theory that our galaxy is but one of billions in the universe and this allows her to rest easy: "Because the real point ... is seeing something bigger. And knowing we're a small part of it, if we're lucky. In the end that is a life well-lived" (54).

Mortality is the common ground where Gunderson's scientists and artists[9] pursue their investigations. It is a space of mystery and demand to which all other experiences of life lead or are built in response. It has the benefit of being brutally factual – we all succumb – and enticingly unknowable. The drive to prolong our time, to avoid/deny this reality shapes many of her character's choices. In *Emilie*, the titular character is brought to life by the theater's power to reanimate. The hypothetical "engine" of *Ada and the Engine*, spins into life as Ada Lovelace dies of cancer, the same disease that takes Henrietta Leavitt, who stands on the bow of death's ocean liner at the end of *Silent Sky*, joined by a lineage of blood and intellectual family members. The theme of legacy echoes from *Background* to *The Catastrophist* as a scientist's professional legacy validates or contrasts with a scientist's familial legacy. In *The Catastrophist*'s final moments, we hear Nathan's heart renewed and its healthy beats mix with those of his wife, his young son, his newborn son and through them he hears the beating of his father's and grandfather's hearts, which fell silent too young. For the unmarried and childless Leavitt, scientific legacy is her family legacy, one that keeps her working through the pain of cancer even as her sister, a composer, encourages her to rest and remember all she has done so far:

> MARGARET: You may not know how you might matter to people right now, and you cannot know how you will matter in the future. But you are *already* connected – and you *already* matter. Because what you do outlasts you. Sometimes.
>
> (54)

Most tellingly, in *Emilie: La Marquise du Châtelet Defends Her Life Tonight*, the battle to prove one's legacy is the title itself. Since Emilie dies at the age of forty-three giving birth to a daughter who herself would live less than two years, Gunderson allows her protagonist the chance to learn that her theories laid the groundwork for Einstein's. The realization that her intellectual progeny provided support for revolutionary physics allows her spirit to rest.

While the contributions of her women protagonists often comprise a footnote or addendum in textbooks and historical accounts, Gunderson's plays provide them a long-deferred recognition. She also employs the theater's tools to illuminate scientific achievements that can benefit all humanity. Each field provides a service to the other:

> Science is great drama: people risking for something they believe in that may sound crazy to other people, something that will create great change at the climactic moment. When the fight is fought, science changes the world; you can't really have a bigger change than that… . All of that makes for really great drama that sticks, that is emotionally interesting and visceral.
>
> (Qtd. in Drostova)

Such stakes mean that endings are key because the "question posed by the story has to have a solution" whether it be "relief or revelation" (Wallace and Campbell). A play's end should offer coherence, catharsis, and possibly a conversation to carry out from the theater venue into the wider world. In this way, even without their direct commission, Gunderson's dramaturgy of biography reflects the Sloan Foundation's central goal: a story that makes an audience feel informed and inspired to go out and seek more information about the person, field, or phenomenon that the play explores.

Learning to Speak in Dialogue

For the conclusion of his 1999 *New York Times* profile of science plays, Robert Meyers interviewed theater artist Peter Brook about possible new encroachments of science into the domain of art. Brook, the child of two scientists, was already well known for lengthy incubations of new work such as *L'homme qui or The Man Who: A Theatrical Research* (1993). Inspired by the then-emerging field of neuroscience and several of physician Oliver Sacks's narrativized case studies collected in *The Man Who Mistook His Wife for a Hat* (1985), Brook spent months researching and rehearsing, creating a script with four actors who play interchanging roles of doctor and patient. Brook seemed to anticipate Meyers's concerns about corollaries of practice between art and science:

> If one takes the theater as being quite simply a microcosm in which you can look at life under a microscope, then in any situation you like, from the most banal to the most exotic, you see a series of processes. But what makes it possible to put those processes into a form that an audience can see? How that can be dramatized is a very difficult question. The fascinating things in science don't necessarily come in an obvious way through human beings.

Perhaps it was a similar realization, that prompted Djerassi to pursue playwriting in the first place as he opines, "In our formal written discourse, we scientists never use the dialogic form—in fact we are not permitted to use it. Yet pedagogically, dialog is frequently more accessible and—let's be frank—also more entertaining" (*An Immaculate Misconception* ix). Under the controlled conditions of scripted theater, the dramatist uses dialogue to both open and productively constrain possibility. *The Man Who* offers extended monologues with the pacing and detail similar to transcriptions from patient records and brief, often indeterminant, scenes depicting characters' behaviors that are in conflict or in concert with physician directives or statements of fact about time, place, and event. Brook portrays the complexity of the conditions diagnosed without any comforting conclusions save for the notion that the boundaries of normative cognitive function are as much socially determined as they are medically defined. The play's title itself is an incomplete sentence, underscoring the very impossibility of certainty when it comes to the brain. There is a man and the interrogative pronoun "who" opens an entire landscape of possibility regarding identity, self-awareness, neurotypical and social expectations of behavior. That openness makes it a transfixing night in the theater. The question for the discipline of neuroscience becomes, is openness enough?

This might also be a question for the discipline of theater. After almost 30 years of Sloan commissions, the limited number of science plays produced for extended runs in the commercial theater would seem to indicate American audiences are reluctant to seek out plays for scientific information. Sloan might also be less directly influential of whether artists write science plays or how new science plays are found and produced by theaters.[10] But there are some promising possibilities. Gunderson's success illustrates that a dramaturgy of biography focused on women scientists can provide both fields with new boosters and acolytes. In the case of S.T.A.G.E., perhaps a melding of a dramaturgy of biography with a dramaturgy of design might produce transdisciplinary forms or, as in *BrainWorks*, an evolution of the scientist character as physician-interlocutor who teaches but also learns from patients. In an age when scientific illiteracy meets active systems of disinformation, it seems unwise to relinquish Djerassi's "science-in-theater" insistence that scientific experts should vet content, if not form. And yet, despite the disparities even in 1999 between STEM and the arts in terms of government funding, educational development, and public respect, Brook waxes rhapsodic about theater's authority as a "two cultures" partner in his interview with Meyers. Asked if he believed playwrights and directors were turning to plays about science because they envied the creative power of scientists, Brook replied "Oh, God, no. I think it's the other way around. I think the scientist is furiously jealous of what for 2,000 years has been the capacity of the imagination to leap into creating. Look how many lives Shakespeare created, and he didn't have any instruments to help." His answer almost anticipates Gunderson's view on theater's power and potential. With recent advancements in artificial intelligence technologies such as DALL·E and ChatGPT, we are entering a new era of scientific incursion into the fields of creativity, one that might upend our previous understandings of the "two cultures" divide. That is material, however, for another book.

Notes

1 For the rest of the chapter, I will use *Art of* to reference this work.
2 In her 2011 article, "Staging Science with Albert Einstein," Zehelein cautions against transposing experimentation from science to theater whole cloth. She cautions that even when scientists within plays invoke the term "experiment," it is an association largely devoid of its scientific context (561).
3 Kawalek does not use the term "rehearsal" and perhaps this is appropriate as S.T.A.G.E. projects do not follow the conventional format of a playwright crafting a script that a production team works to realize.
4 Initial performances took place at St. Louis's Sheldon Concert Hall in 2014; then the show went on a brief tour and was filmed for St. Louis's PBS affiliate, Channel 9, in 2015.
5 Celia Wren quotes Gunderson in a profile for the *Washington Post* likening theater to "an experiment to 'test the capacity of human feeling.'"
6 Gunderson used similar language in her 2011 "Play Math: A Secret Guide to Dramatic Structure," workshop description on the event's ticketing site.
7 When citing *Background*, I refer to the version I first read published in a 2009 issue of a now-shuttered literary journal, *Isotope*, not the version that can be found in *Deepen the Mystery: Science and the South on Stage, a Collection of Plays by Lauren Gunderson.*
8 In another binary composition, Maria is more measured in her approach, Brightman more erratic and flamboyant.

9 I use "art" here because poetry, painting, photography, and music populate Gunderson's plays even more than theater making or theater going save *The Book of Will*, which is about Shakespeare.

10 The New Play Exchange allows playwrights to upload scenes or full drafts of work for memberships of $12 or $18/year and identify their work through subject or genre tags. Readers subscribe for $10 or $12/year to search this database for specific writers' work or to find work searching such descriptions. A broad search in May 2021 for "science" produced 36 pages of results with 15 titles per page.

References

Ahl, Jonathan. "BrainWorks Production Takes Neuroscience out of Surgical Room and onto Theater Stage." *St. Louis on the Air*, 9 July 2019. *iHeart Podcasts.* iheart.com/podcast/269-st-louis-on-the-air-30712376/episode/brainworks-production-takes-neuroscience-out-of-46782356/.

Barnett, Laura. "Interview with Carl Djerassi." *The Guardian*, 8 Sept. 2012. www.theguardian.com/stage/2012/sep/09/carl-djerassi-insufficiency-play-interview.

Bauld, Andrew. "Artists, Scientists Discover New Perspectives Through Collaboration." *UChicagoNews*, 7 Apr.2017. www.news.uchicago.edu/story/artists-scientists-discover-new-perspectives-through-collaboration.

"BrainWorks: The Theatre of Neuroscience." *Nine PBS*, St. Louis. 2020. www.ninepbs.org/brainworks/.

Brook, Peter, and Marie-Helene Estienne. *The Man Who: A Theatrical Research*. Methuen, 2002.

Campos, Liliane. "Science in Contemporary British Theatre: A Conceptual Approach." *Interdisciplinary Science Reviews*, vol. 38, no. 4, 2013, pp. 295–305. doi:10.1179/0308018813Z.00000000060.

Deni, Laura. "Science Takes Center Stage." *BroadwaytoVegas.com*, 25 Feb.2007. www.broadwaytovegas.com/February25,2007.html.

Dezell, Maureen. "Setting Dramas of Love and Loss in the World of Mathematics." *Boston Globe*, 27 Jan.2002. *ProQuest*. https://www.proquest.com/newspapers/setting-dramas-love-loss-world-mathematics/docview/405437377/se-2?accountid=10598.

Djerassi, Carl. *An Immaculate Misconception: Sex in an Age of Mechanical Reproduction*. Imperial College Press, 2000.

Djerassi, Carl. *Chemistry in Theatre: Insufficiency, Phallacy or Both*. Imperial College Press, 2012.

Drostova, Lisa. "Science on Stage." *Theatre Bay Area Online*. 2 Jul.2015. www.theatrebayarea.org/news/239629/.

"Eureka Stories: The Power for Putting Science Center-Stage." The Aspen Institute, 30 Mar.2021. *YouTube*. youtube.com/live/gE_ZBJ5_oWg?feature=share.

Foster, Catherine. "Growing a Culture if One Foundation Has Its Way, Copenhagen and A Beautiful Mind Won't Be the Only Science You See on Stage and Screen." *Boston Globe*, 26 Jan.2003. https://www.proquest.com/

newspapers/growing-culture-if-one-foundation-has-way/docview/405503197/se-2?accountid=10598.

Grünzweig, Walter. *The Sciartist: Carl Djerassi's Science-in-Literature in Transatlantic and Interdisciplinary Contexts.* LIT, 2012.

Gunderson, Lauren. *Ada and the Engine.* Dramatists, 2018.

Gunderson, Lauren. *Background. Isotope: A Journal of Literary Nature and Science Writing*, vol. 7, no. 1, 2009. Department of English, Utah State University, pp. 3–14.

Gunderson, Lauren. *Emilie: La Marquise du Châtelet Defends Her Life Tonight*. Samuel French, 2010.

Gunderson, Lauren. *I & You*. Playscripts, 2014.

Gunderson, Lauren. *Leap. Deepen the Mystery: Science and the South Onstage, a Collection of Plays by Lauren Gunderson*. iUniverse. 2005, pp. 1–142.

Gunderson, Lauren. "Play Math: A Secret Guide to Dramatic Structure." Playwrights Foundation, Apr.–May 2011. Brown Paper Tickets, www.brownpapertickets.com/event/145069.

Gunderson, Lauren. "Science Plays Come of Age." *The Scientist.com*, 27 Jul. 2006. the-scientist.com/daily-news/science-plays-come-of-age-47362.

Gunderson, Lauren. *Silent Sky*. Dramatists, 2015.

Gunderson, Lauren. *The Catastrophist*. Premiere Production Draft. 2021.

Gunderson, Lauren. "The Ending of the Play's the Thing." *Wall Street Journal*, 26 Nov.2011. https://www.proquest.com/historical-newspapers/ending-plays-thing/docview/2729897645/se-2?accountid=10598.

Handelsman, Jo, and Megan Smith. "*Stem for All.*" 16 Feb.2016. obamawhitehouse.archives.gov/blog/2016/02/11/stem-all.

Henerson, Evan. "A Winning Construct: David Auburn's Play *Proof* Began with a Simple Idea, and Then One Thing Followed from Another." *Daily News* [Los Angeles], 4 June 2002. https://www.proquest.com/newspapers/winning-construct-david-auburns-play-proof-began/docview/282216370/se-2?accountid=10598.

Horwitz, Simi. "Science Takes to the Stage." *Backstage Magazine*, vol. 44, no. 10, 7 Mar. 2003. https://www.proquest.com/trade-journals/science-takes-stage/docview/221127636/se-2?accountid=10598.

Institute for Molecular Engineering. "3Q Quarterly Report: Coming of Age During the Molecular Engineering Revolution."University of Chicago, 2017. www.pme.uchicago.edu/sites/default/files/2019-10/2017_IME_3Q_Report.pdf.

Kawalek, Nancy. "Blurring the Boundaries between Science and Art." TEDx UChicago, 4 July 2016. *TEDx Talks YouTube*. youtu.be/l-vw0jStK34.

Kazzazi, Seyedeh Anahit. "Performing Science: New Physics and Contemporary British and American Science Plays." Dissertation, University of Sussex, 3 May 2017. sro.sussex.ac.uk/id/eprint/67576/.

Kazzazi, Seyedeh Anahit. "The Anatomy of the Science Play." *New Theatre Quarterly*, vol. 33, no. 4, 2017, pp. 333–344. doi:10.1017/S0266464X17000471.

L.A. Theatre Works. *The Relativity Series: Science Themed Plays*. 2017. latw.org/relativity-series.

Lee, Ashley, "Lauren Gunderson's New Play Is about Virologist Nathan Wolfe. Or Is It?" *Los Angeles Times*, 4 Feb. 2021. www.latimes.com/entertainment-arts/story/2021-02-04/lauren-gunderson-catastrophist-nathan-wolfe.

Leuthardt, Eric C., MD, and Albert H. Kim, MD, hosts. *The Brain Coffee Podcast*. 3 seasons, 2018–2020, Apple Podcasts. *iTunes* app.

Li, Annie. "Alum Most Produced Living Playwright in U.S." *The Emory Wheel*, 24 Oct. 2018. www.emorywheel.com/gunderson/.

Liwag, Andra Parrish. "Playwright John Walch's Work Featured in 'BrainWorks: The Theatre of Neuroscience.'" *University of Arkansas News*, 18 July 2019. www.news.uark.edu/articles/49518/playwright-john-walch-s-work-featured-in-brainworks-the-theatre-of-neuroscience-.

Marks, Peter. "Now Hear This! Playwrights Are Making Theater for the Ears. Yes, That's a Thing." *Washington Post*, 26 Mar. 2019. www.washingtonpost.com/entertainment/theater_dance/now-hear-this-playwrights-are-making-theater-for-the-ears-yes-thats-a-thing/2019/11/26/76bfb9a2-0ed7-11ea-b0fc-62cc38411ebb_story.html.

Meyers, Robert. "Science, Infiltrating the Stage, Puts Life Under the Microscope." *New York Times*, 5 Dec. 1999. https://www.proquest.com/historical-newspapers/science-infiltrating-stage-puts-life-under/docview/109995318/se-2?accountid=10598.

"MTC Announces 6 New Recipients of Sloan Commissions." *American Theater*, 18 May 2020. www.americantheatre.org/2020/05/18/mtc-announces-6-new-recipients-of-sloan-commissions/.

National New Play Network. *New Play Exchange*. 2016. newplayexchange.org.

NOVA. "Einstein's Big Idea: Ancestors of E=MC^2." *PBS*, Jun. 2005. www.pbs.org/wgbh/nova/einstein/ance-sq.html.

Overbye, Dennis. "Lab Coat Chic: The Arts Embrace Science." *New York Times*, 28 Jan. 2003. https://www.proquest.com/newspapers/lab-coat-chic-arts-embrace-science/docview/432283826/se-2?accountid=10598.

Powell, Corey S. "Science Acts Out." *Discover*, vol. 21, no. 8, Aug. 2000, pp. 86–88.

Rabinowitz, Chloe. "Ensemble Studio Theatre Announces 2020–21 EST/Sloan Project Commissions." *Broadwayworld.com*, 27 May 2020. www.broadwayworld.com/off-off-broadway/article/Ensemble-Studio-Theatre-Announces-2020-21-ESTSloan-Project-Commissions-20200527.

Schwartz, Brian. "Communicating Science Through the Performing Arts." *Interdisciplinary Science Reviews*, vol. 39, no. 3, 2014, pp. 275–289. doi:10.1179/0308018814Z.00000000089.

Sloan Foundation. "*Grants Database*." 2022. www.sloan.org/grants-database.

S.T.A.G.E.: Scientists, Technologists & Artists Generating Exploration. University of Chicago. n.d. www.stage.pme.uchicago.edu/.

S.T.A.G.E. Collaboratory: Scientists, Technologists & Artists Generating Exploration. University of California, Santa Barbara. 2005–2015. www.stage.cnsi.ucsb.edu/collaboratory/.

Tran, Diep. "The Top 20 Most-Produced Playwrights of the 2017–18 Season." *American Theatre*, vol. 34, no. 8, Oct. 2017, pp. 42–43.

Wallace, Christina, and Cate Scott Campbell, hosts. "The Science of Drama (Lauren Gunderson)." *The Limit Does Not Exist*. Season 1, episode 17. 28 Oct. 2016. *iTunes* app.

Weinert-Kendt, Rob. "Lauren Gunderson on *I and You*, a Play with an Explosive Twist." *New York Times*, 10 Jan. 2018. www.nytimes.com/2016/01/10/theater/lauren-gunderson-on-i-and-you-a-play-with-an-explosive-twist.html.

Wren, Celia. "Dramatist Inserts Science in the Spotlight." *Washington Post*, 12 Dec. 2019. https://www.proquest.com/newspapers/dramatist-inserts-science-spotlight/docview/2326321053/se-2?accountid=10598.

Zehelein, Eva-Sabine. *Science: Dramatic. Science Plays in America and Great Britain, 1990–2007*. Universitätsverlag Winter, 2009.

Zehelein, Eva-Sabine. "*Staging It: Bridging the Two Cultures? Mick Gordon, Paul Broks: On Ego*." The 11th International Conference of ISSEI, University of Helsinki, July 28–August 2, 2008. helda.helsinki.fi/bitstream/handle/10138/15321/55_Zehelein.pdf?sequence=1.

Zehelein, Eva-Sabine. "Staging Science with Albert Einstein." *Restoring the Mystery of the Rainbow: Literatures Refraction of Science*, edited by Valeria Tinkler-Vilani and C.C. Barfoot. Brill, 2011, pp. 549–566. https://doi.org/10.1163/9789401200011_030.

2 Dramaturgy of Interdependence

Every Play a Climate Change Play[1]

In my first offering of a *Performing Science* class in 2011, one student offered a theory for why there was a growth of arts projects focused on the environment, particularly global warming.[2] For him, environmental science was a "crisis science" with strong foundations in biology, chemistry, and physics, but the employment of its research findings toward public policy goals pulled it problematically into the realm of qualitative methods and communication tools such as storytelling and artistic representation. A decade later, headlines flash across my smartphone: an "all-time heat wave" across the western United States and Canada cooks marine life within their ocean habitats; videos from New York and China show commuters wading through waist-high storm and sewage water flushed into subway lines due to the frequency of inland flooding from cloudburst storms; and an "eye of fire" caused by a gas leak from an underwater pipeline burns on the water's surface in the Gulf of Mexico. I sometimes wonder how that student might frame environmental scientists' multidisciplinary work on such crises today. Playwright Caridad Svich, who inspires the title of this section, poses the question of crisis directly to theater artists: "When the world is in multiple levels of sociopolitical and ecological disrepair, what kind of theater, if any, can be made as an act of potential regeneration, and what could be its modes of transformation?" (58). Svich finds the term "eco-drama" lacking, as it can designate a "niche" genre focused primarily on content. Instead, in a 2021 conversation with Pedro de Senna of *Lend Me Your Ears*, she notes that "everything we do when we make art, and specifically theatre, because we're theatre-makers, has to be eco-conscious, you know, because we're responding to it, we're in response to our environment." Consequently, she argues, "all plays written in the last fifty

DOI: 10.4324/9781003150848-3

years are climate change plays" (57). The discipline of environmental science shares a similar embeddedness; it is comprised of interdisciplinary practices and domains of inquiry and yet faces criticism for simultaneously too much or too little specificity in its findings as those findings tend to reflect the interconnectedness of systems and impacts that require both individual and systemic changes to prevent or stem current and anticipated effects.

At first glance, those who chart taxonomies of science plays do not appear to include environmental science as science. In her *Science: Dramatic* chronicle of twentieth-century science plays in the United States and United Kingdom, Zehelein makes only a passing mention of Henrik Ibsen's *An Enemy of the People* in which a local physician struggles against governmental and business interests to expose and correct the contamination of the health baths that are a tourist centerpiece of his town's economy. The plot is less focused on pollution chemistry or groundwater conservation in favor of dramatizing the valiant ethics of a heroic doctor who forfeits his public and private position for the sake of the truth. Shepherd-Barr, whose *Science on Stage* volume predates Zehelein's study by three years and extends the timeline of science plays back much further, includes *Enemy* in her chapter on physician protagonists, using a logic similar to the one in this book as she carves out medicine as a unique branch of science with which audience members have more experience than particle physics or geology. In the epilogue of her 2015 book, *Theatre and Evolution from Ibsen to Beckett*, Shepherd-Barr explores plays that anticipate or represent the Anthropocene (273–74), those that depict "retro-Victorianism" (Mary Vingoe's *Living Curiosities; or, What You Will*), genetic futurism (*Ex Vivo/In Vitro* devised by Jean-Francois Peyret and Alain Prochaintz) and interspeciality (Terry Johnson's *Cries from the Mammal House*; David Greig's *Outlying Islands*). She characterizes these pieces as representing a (possible) next stage in the evolutionary timeline of human development and theatrical storytelling that centers "crisis, regression, and stasis" (283).

Finding environmental science as a whole "underrepresented" and "underthematized on the Western Stage" (Arons and May 1), scholars Theresa J. May and Wendy Arons created Earth Matters on Stage (EMOS), an effort that has included a play competition and festival to workshop and showcase new plays and whose scholarship has grown to fill special issue journals and essay collections. May examines EMOS's winners and participants in her own work on "ecodramaturgy," which she defines as the "critical lens [that] examines the role of theater in the face of rising ecology crises, foregrounding the material ecologies represented on stage" (May 4). Ecodramaturgy brings an environmental eye to plays that, to quote Svich, "respond to their environment" within the stage worlds they create, whether they address environmental science directly or not. For May, ecodramaturgy presents an opportunity for theater makers to work toward environmentally aware goals such as countering historical mythologies (such as Manifest Destiny) and linear narratives (with a skew toward individual redemption) that problematically occlude the relationships scientific and artistic advancements have with extractive economies.

This chapter identifies a **dramaturgy of interdependence** in work where theatrical world building meets environmental science, placing May's ecodramaturgy in conversation with Australian playwright Paul Brown's notions of theater as knowledge building and the truth of phenomena as something negotiated through acts of making, experience, and reception. From here, the chapter examines two meta-theatrical plays: *(Not) Water* by Sheila Callaghan and Daniella Topol and *The Great Immensity* by The Civilians' Steve Cosson and Michael Friedman. These pieces depict a broad array of given circumstances particularly around environmental catastrophe and employ a range of theatrical devices to convey the scale, pace, and entangled dimensions of the current existential threat of climate change. The question of whether such pieces invigorate or confound disciplinary partnerships with science is something explored here and in the next chapter as imperatives shift from information delivery to participatory research. The chapter concludes with the discussion of *Frozen Fluid* by Fly Jamerson in which the playwright presses the boundaries of theatrical form to navigate a troubled Anthropocene.[3] Jamerson links earth-shattering experiences to gender-affirmation processes, demonstrating that even shared attitudes and collaborations across art and science comprise only partial webs of knowledge. The future-oriented nature of the plays in this chapter provides opportunities to prepare audiences to think in ways that are vital to comprehend the events ahead, ones in which humans have already played a key role and ones in which recognizing our ecological embeddedness is essential for a fully inclusive future.

EMOS Foundations

Most of May's career has been dedicated to connecting community-based, socially conscious performance and sustainable (or "green") theater practices[4] that model interdependency so that theater might play a role in assessing the "consequences of human action," ecologically, relationally, and emotionally (May 3). In her 2020 monograph, *Earth Matters on Stage: Ecology and Environment in American Theater*, she articulates a cautiously optimistic vision for theater as a research and a civic practice, while also acknowledging the all-too-complicit role the theater industry and discipline have played in propping up "Manifest Destiny, white supremacy, and extractive capitalism" (5). To redirect this trajectory, May offers "ecodramaturgy" as a multipronged "praxis" methodology steeped in "critical, self-reflexive awareness about how we represent, discuss, and frame history" (8; 4–5). May selects an array of texts from nineteenth-century theater history when a new era of settler colonialism was in full swing at the same time the United States was codifying its mythological foundations and representational languages. Many of the plays she discusses do not depict scientists or scientific research, but they do show the effects of modernity, capitalism, and colonization forces made possible by scientific discovery and innovation.

May presents ecodramaturgy as a lens for creating work that takes up issues of material production and makes "the best use of the ways of knowing at the heart of theatrical practice – embodied exploration, story sharing, communal creation, imaginative experimentation, and the palpable immediacy of being together." Ecodramaturgy, for May, encompasses an array of theatrical work from the past, present, and future, and she offers theater as a collaborative, embodied research partner to civic and scientific entities who want to address our current "environmental crisis" and who believe that stories are "ecological forces that inscribe both the land and our bodies." Such a vision argues that by crafting new stories that "reflect reciprocity with the planet" theater can provide "nourishment for our species and for the nonhuman communities that share this home planet with us" as well as tools to "illuminate, inspire, and actualize an ecologically just and interdependent future" (13, 14).

In many ways, May's invocation of theater as civic engine for generosity and collaboration echoes similar arguments from Paul Brown, an artist and educator at the University of New South Wales (UNSW). In the late 1970s during the final years of his PhD in geology at UNSW, Brown founded a political theater company with other alumni. Death Defying Theater (which later became Urban Theatre Projects) devised work out of a range of research processes and a stated resistance to the commercial theater. In the early 1980s, Brown and his collective built a catalog of "art and working life" projects supported by the Australia Council and trade unions in an effort "to jointly fund cultural activities in accessible and relevant contexts for working people" (Guthrie 170). Scholars credit Brown with helping bring documentary/verbatim theater practices to Australia and almost all of these early projects connected labor issues with environmental issues, such as *Coal Town* (1983) about the mining community at Collinsville, North Queensland; the site-specific community pageant, *Murray River Story* (1988); and *Aftershocks* (1991), which recounts the destruction of the Newcastle Workers Club in a 1989 earthquake. Writing about *Aftershocks*, Brown calls the script, built from interviews with union members who had been absented from mainstream news reports, a "negotiation towards a truth," the "construct of a particular process" that produces that truth from community participation, dramaturgical choices, and production techniques that foreground the mechanics of such a synergy (*Verbatim* 40).

Brown's interdisciplinary authority rests on techniques that are informed by formal training in science and informal training in theater arts. He uses investigatory/research techniques common to documentary and devised theater for a variety of reasons, including a reliance on the situated truth of experience to humanize the so-called objective truth of science. Brown argues that embodied arts practices like theater making, particularly that made with community participation, provide similar experiences and stages of knowing as the scientific method: "observation … theory-making and induction … and deduction and problem solving." By extension, the activity of research/rehearsal/performance "becomes a representative exercise, delivering many of the objectives of other participatory processes" such as policy debate, political decision making ("Ecological Knowledge in Community Theater" 6). This is community participation broadly characterized as it includes artists, scientists, non-artists, and non-scientists who provide personal stories or accounts through writing or other means of recording, share official records or information gained through a range of expertise, and sometimes act as performers or participate in the theatrical product in capacities beyond audience members.

Brown elevates the artist in these collaborations because they culminate in creative, public performances. Artists are best equipped to navigate the range of participatory influences at work in such presentations and, as such,

> may systematize their observations and organize their knowledge building processes using approaches which are "just as intentional, just as institutionalized, just as governed by set protocols

> as is the production of scientific knowledge." … Artists then invite the public to test the creative idea in their own life world, and this parallels the testing and making of everyday decisions based on scientific theories (deduction).
>
> ("Ecological Knowledge in Community Theater" 6–7)[5]

Brown acknowledges the limits of his analogy for many scientists who would argue the arts only provide "contextualized" knowledge. Still, he insists that "the arts have a role in establishing sites for (rational) knowledge production and that when that knowledge is made it can assist in policy and decision making" (7). These are elements sorely needed to fill a "deficit of workable approaches to environmental protection" and provide "innovative techniques of grappling with environmental problems" (2). The key element to achieve this promised complex and communal approach is participation across a range of experiences, expertise, and engagement. Brown makes a case for feeling and emotion as essential to knowledge and to the actions required to understand and to change an unsustainable status quo: "the arts … possess knowledge-making functions which are related to the way we make meaning out of the world and to the need for problem solving in a world made complex and uncertain by modern day environmental risk" (9).

It Starts with a Storm

Uncertainty and risk also surround theatrical endeavors. *(Not) Water*'s collaborative authors – surrealist playwright Sheila Callaghan and director Daniella Topol – planned to write a play about Hurricane Katrina titled *WATER* (Collins-Hughes). The Category 5 storm that made landfall in Louisiana during the last week of August 2005 was described in *Times-Picayune* headlines and by the National Weather Service as "catastrophic" and a range of problematic decisions enacted at the state and federal level made Katrina's environmental and infrastructure damage significantly worse in the months and years that followed.[6] Callaghan had written a monologue about Katrina, and from that seed, they imagined an integrated development process with designers and dramaturgs to take advantage of the newly opened (in 2006) "technology-driven performance space," 3LD Art & Technology Center in Lower Manhattan (Tran).

In November 2012, however, a scheduled workshop of *WATER* was caught in the aftermath of Hurricane Sandy, which flooded not only the hosting 3LD but many other nearby performance spaces as well as the financial district, plunging most of Lower Manhattan into darkness, grinding transit systems to a halt, closing schools and hospitals (Gibbons).[7] Another five years would pass before the play, which had become *(Not) Water*, was presented to the public in June 2017. The play anchored Works on Water's inaugural month of site-specific performance events[8] that used 3LD as home base with central curatorial and funding support by New Georges, an institution known since the early 1990s for its support of new work by women writers. *(Not) Water* premiered three years after the first national news stories about contaminated drinking water in Flint, Michigan, in the same month that then-president Donald J. Trump announced the United States was leaving the Paris Climate Accord, and in the first month of the 2017 hurricane season when three storms (Harvey, Irma, and Maria) made landfall, causing 3,500 deaths and about $300 billion in damage to the United States and its territories (Loop News).

In an interview with the *New York Times*, the artists acknowledged how environmental events changed the show sometimes at a dizzying pace (Collins-Hughes). The parenthetical *(Not)* of the title serves multiple purposes. The play is *not* the original piece that Callaghan and Topol started creating in 2006. The water we meet in the play will *not* be a person. Finally, what we encounter in the performance is imagined chaos that happens *without* water, either water that is safe to consume or without water at all as it is wasted, polluted, or simply used up without any new sources. I attended a performance of *(Not) Water* and my analysis is based on both that performance experience with direct quotes from the unpublished script courtesy of Sheila Callaghan.

(Not) Water: Interactivity, Ingestion, Immersion

Callaghan decided on a meta-theatrical frame where the characters of "Not Sheila and DT (and their design team) try to make a play about water," including script revisions made just months earlier (Collins-Hughes). "We don't want a polemic. This is about humans, not issues!" Not Sheila exclaims (30) but who are *they* to be telling this story in the first place? Although it might have come late in the development process, this real person as character construction allows the artists the opportunity for self-critique and critiques of multiple intervening influences (collaborators, critics, funders, other experts) to illustrate just how intertwined a story of humans and water must be. Water in *(Not) Water* is given form by a voice broadcast over the sound system. Water as voice-over is our guide through the immersive, interactive performance and it orients audience improvisation.[9] Prior to entering the performance space, the script calls for audience members to encounter "a fishbowl, pens and paper." Directions hand-printed on a large sticky pad outside the theater doors at 3LD read:

> [On this paper write] your most vivid/meaningful/important/memorable experience with water, either from childhood or recently. Write legibly, using complete sentences. Tell it like a bedtime story. Then place your story into the bowl.
>
> (1)

Although the audience does not know it at the time, these stories will comprise the majority of *(Not) Water*'s part 3.

At 3LD, installations from other Works on Water artists were part of the stage area for patrons to engage preshow and at other times during the monthlong festival. The art pieces shared the performance's makeshift and minimalist stagecraft with support from complex soundscapes, lighting, and projection media.[10] For the 2017 performances of *(Not) Water*, everything appeared to inhabit the same carefully constructed world as if audience members were the last part of a community pageant waiting for us to take our places.[11] Capacity was limited to around 50 spectators, making it relatively easy to engage in collective action: moving our chairs around the room in part 1, selecting from pool toys offered in part 3, hunkering into the smaller performance spaces for part 2.

A *New York Times* preview of *(Not) Water* identifies the piece as an "eco-play" (Collins-Hughes), but it is more aptly described by a *Times* reviewer as an "assemblage" of scenes (Soloski) that its creators' doppelgängers – Not Sheila, DT, and Designer Ethan, Designer Mike, Designer Carmen – draft and redraft as they cover ten years of investigating water, trying to "turn something we take for granted into something we hold sacred" (9). In part 1, we careen with the cast from one tone, one narrative device, one organizing theme to another while the playwrights seem to change dialogue, collaborators to debate aesthetic choices, and actors to receive direction all in the moment. We watch the characters wrestle with tricky ethics, confronted with events "ripped from the headlines," and their own limited perspectives as middle-class, mostly white, U.S. citizens in an environmental crisis. We move with them from the initial inspiration (Hurricane Katrina) through thorny questions regarding lack of focus, lack scientific rigor, and lack of funding and space until Hurricane Sandy lands on their doorsteps, and then the election of Donald Trump as president, which brings us to the present of the June 2017 performance.

Before anything like clarity emerges, alarms sound and a presumed stage manager evacuates us from the central performance space. As we exit, we are randomly[12] divided into two groups: one pulled into the venue's bathroom by Dr. Grace Sterner, "the Scientist," the others descending a back stairwell into a space set up like the "small kitchen of an abandoned restaurant" where we meet an unnamed "Crafty Cook" (Callaghan 53). Whereas part 1 is a chaotic carnival of styles, sights, and sounds, the monologue vignettes of part 2 take place in the pregnant pause of an apocalyptic landscape that has followed "Hurricane Gwyneth" whose advent, we learn, ended part 1 (59).

In the bathroom, Dr. Sterner quizzes her gathered group about the state of the outside world and offers us "free water" served from what the stage directions describe as "a high-tech looking filter" since "assholes are selling bottled water for twenty bucks outside" (Callaghan 59–60). In the kitchen, our host, a dishwasher of an abandoned restaurant, has posted a "free food" sign on the door, even though he is not the chef/owner, nor does he have any food to share. Sterner is waiting for her husband and business partner, Doug, to find her. Luckily, she has their company's key asset with her: a portable water filter, the "Hydra Criterion One," strong and safe enough to transform even human urine into potable water. "Crafty" never identifies himself (one only learns his name from the script) and tells us he has not seen "a living person in four days," existing on "expired peach yogurt" and busying himself with a new idea that just might help this broken world, and make him rich: "spongy, white cubes [of powdered crickets] with the texture of gluten-free bread" supplemented with dropper filled with a scent of homemade pancakes (70–72).

Part 2 also tests the parameters of interactivity established in part 1 when audience members were asked to write down a short story, read from newspapers, move our chairs, and follow emergency directions. Now we are offered items to eat and drink. These are things that look recognizable but proffered within a context where we might worry about the motivations of our hosts. It is a delicate balance that risks exploding the "trick" of each scene, where an adventurous participant might break the illusion by reacting with horror, panic, or anger to the idea of having swallowed a stranger's filtered urine or consumed hand-processed insects. It is also an attempt to simulate under duress decision-making circumstances without placing the audience in actual danger.

The Tiniest Myth, the Largest Leap

The Voice of Water ends part 2 by giving a Land Acknowledgment invoking the city's 520 miles of coastline and the first given names (e. g., *Lenapehoking, Kapsee, Shatemuc*) for the Hudson and East Rivers and the place where they meet, Battery Park, all within walking distance from the theater space. "You are surrounded by water," the Voice tells us. "Please keep this in mind as you exit into the hallway, walk ten paces towards the double doors, enter the theatre, and choose a quiet place to rest" (69). We are directed back to the space of part 1, which has been transformed into a landscape of inflated pool floats of all shapes, sizes, and colors with some beach chairs available for those who do not wish to/could not lie down. With this arrangement, the Voice of Water's invocation to rest was taken by most attendees of the June 2017 performance as an opportunity to recline and either close their eyes or look up at the ceiling, which was a sea of lights, color, and netting that held hundreds of captured plastic bottles. Arrayed on objects usually for keeping above the water, it feels like we are suspended underneath, a literal shift in perspective.

The fishbowl from the lobby is passed around and we are asked to take a story and read it to ourselves. After a time, the Voice of Water reminds us to "look around. Someone in this room wrote the story you hold" and if so moved, we are invited to raise our hand and a microphone is brought so we can read the story slip to the group (56). This is that elusive, golden moment in the theater where a group of strangers becomes, briefly, a community. We might have been on our way to this relationship in part 2, but the unsettled context means we would have united around horror or terror. Here, the invitation and environment are gentle, and even as some stories convey grief and fear, they are spoken with relative emotional detachment, reminiscent of the random selection of audience members reading from the newspapers in part 1.

After the flow of volunteers trickles to a stop, the Voice of Water thanks us "for sharing your stories about … *me*" and asks us to end our experience with the "smallest [story about water] that connects you to me on the inside." It is in this moment where the risky ingestion moments of part 2 may resonate. "I am the tiniest myth," the Voice of Water says, asking us to repeat this phrase with her. She continues,

> I'm your sweat
> Your tears
> Your saliva

Your pee
I am you.
(57)

Having passed through the play's three parts of representation, consumption, and meditation, *(Not) Water*'s goal "to turn something we take for granted into something we hold sacred" (9) is made manifest by enlisting the audience's stories to reconnect with the resource of water. This is not action at the level of "people are gonna walk outta here prepared to change the world" as Not Sheila dreamed but in the more subtle way encouraged by the Voice of Water's introduction in part 1:

> Think about the last bottle of water you drank. Conjure it in your mind… . Picture yourself drinking as much as you can… . How delightful and pure. Does it not feel wonderful to pour something so precious into your body?
>
> (10)

We are it and it is us. With such a visceral reminder of our interdependence, how could we not be on the lookout for ways to protect our water, as doing so also protects ourselves?

(Not) Water premiered within an environmental arts festival; however, to classify it as a site-specific work seems inaccurate. It remains to be seen how the script might be received outside of Lower Manhattan and the surrounding New York City where its only production grew. It might become a work more read more than performed, another trend that marks science plays. For unpublished work to circulate, however, even as a teaching tool, depends on networks of educators with direct connections to playwrights and playwrights willing to allow consumption without production.[13] Consequently, *(Not) Water*'s specific experimentation regarding interactivity and immersion remains widely untested save for how in 2017 it anchored the work of other artists engaging participatory, embodied dimensions of environmentally focused performance and the ways it echoes and expands a lineage of science scripts about elements vital to human life: air, earth, and water.

Of Contingencies and Well-Made Plans

For the 2009–2010 academic year, director/writer Steve Cosson and composer/lyricist Michael Friedman served as visiting professors at Princeton's Environmental Institute (or PEI, now the High Meadows

Environmental Institute) and guests of the Princeton Atelier at the Lewis Center for the Arts. These cofounders of The Civilians, a group that pursues the "creative investigation of actual experience," were taking early steps on a new work titled *The Great Immensity* about global climate change. Cosson and Friedman had already traveled to Barro Colorado Island in the Panama Canal, which the Smithsonian Tropical Research Institute calls the "most intensively studied tropical forest in the world."[14] They had visited Churchill, Manitoba, Canada, known for its polar bear tourist industry and the Churchill Northern Studies Centre, a field station located at the meeting point of three biomes – marine, northern boreal forest, and tundra – critical to understanding climate change impacts.[15] Using the company's core approach, described by Friedman in a 2006 article as "performance based on actual experience (whether through interviews, research, or other investigation) that is grounded in popular styles and cabaret" (324) resulting in a "pastiche" form (325) that is "fun, and upsetting, professional but not smooth, unexpected but not esoteric" (326), the pair integrated interviews conducted in the field with "botanists, paleontologists, climatologists, indigenous community leaders, polar bear tour guides, and trappers" with those from PEI faculty experts: evolutionary biologists, ecologists, geoscientists, mechanical engineers, and climate policy authorities (Peters). The April 2010 work-in-progress showing offered a script centered on twin sisters – Phyllis and Polly – and the range of characters encountered as Phyllis traverses the North American continent searching for Polly, a photojournalist, who has disappeared while in Panama in the time leading up to another global climate summit of world leaders.

A few months later, *Broadway World* ran a press release touting The Civilian's award of a $700,000 grant from the National Science Foundation (NSF) to continue developing *The Great Immensity* for production and a possible national tour. The announcement emphasized the company's previous successful plays built from "real life topics," such as *This Beautiful City* (about the rise and fall of Colorado megachurch pastor Ted Haggard) and *In the Footprint: The Battle over Atlantic Yards* (about gentrification in Brooklyn). The news of this award quickly spread in theater circles due to its size and because it was given to a professional theater company not aligned with a major research university.[16] In his coverage of the award, *New York Times* theater critic Jason Zinoman characterized it as the company's graduation to credibility similar to "passionate long-form journalism," anticipating more new productions focused on "ambitious major issues." The funds was given under the NSF's Advancing Informal

STEM Learning (AISL) category, which articulates goals similar to those that might motivate a Sloan commission: "To help the public better appreciate how science studies the Earth's biosphere and to promote an inquisitive curiosity about our place in the natural world" with specific ambitions "to create and evaluate a new model for how theater can increase public awareness, knowledge, and engagement with important science-related societal issues" and provide deliverables, including "online content, podcasts, and videos" that would accompany "community education and outreach efforts in each community where the play is staged."[17]

Between Cosson's and Friedman's residency at Princeton and *The Great Immensity*'s world premiere at the Kansas City Repertory Theater in February 2012, the production's most visible footprint could be found on TheGreatImmensity.org. As snapshots of the 2011–2018 website are now only accessible via archive.org, a reminder of the extended ephemerality of performance documentation in the digital age, I rely on its remnants (such as Vimeo clips on The Civilians' main website), my own recollection of the multiple visits I made between 2011 and 2015, and the description and evaluation given in the company's report to the NSF.[18] The pages' ample content connects multiple strains of scientific research to policy proposals and personal testimonials (many that resonate within the script) and global climate resources. A treasure trove for visitors, the website centered the play's development alongside current scientific research intertwining both for a fuller picture of human impacts, interpretations and representations of those impacts, and proposed and imagined interventions.

We Are All Panamanian

As is common in new play development processes, there were differences in the script seen in Kansas City in 2012 and that which premiered in New York City in 2014. One of the most significant shifts seems to have come just weeks before the opening at The Public Theater.[19] Preview publicity in the *New York Times* as late as April 16, 2014 describes the plot as a mystery, following "a woman trying to find out what happened to a friend who disappeared while on assignment for a television show." By the time of preview performances in New York, Cosson and Friedman had recalibrated the plot away from one sister's search (Phyllis) for her twin (Polly, both played by a single actor) to center on Phyllis, now a middle-class housewife searching for her missing nature documentarian husband, Karl, who has disappeared in the months leading up to the 2015 Climate Conference in

Paris.[20] Since The Public Theater's production was built from the script version available on Cosson's New Play Exchange page, which is the one referenced by reviewers of the New York production and from which the songs were recorded for the soundtrack, it is the one from which I draw my analysis.[21]

The story is told from multiple perspectives along slightly different timelines: Phyllis, as she retraces her missing husband Karl's steps; Karl, a "maker of TV nature shows" like *Shark Week* as he tries to make a different kind of story about the natural world (Cosson and Friedman 2, 9), leading him to Julie, a teenage climate activist with ties to a network of activist hackers; and the array of scientists, policymakers, and local inhabitants of Panama and Canada Karl and Phyllis meet. The music in both the Kansas City and New York productions exemplifies The Civilians postmodern Brechtian style with songs across a range of styles (ballads, torch songs, barbershop quartet, even more standard musical theater recitative) punctuating scenes or sometimes fracturing a moment's coherence. Even the titular cargo ship, *The Great Immensity*, has its own ballad and role in the plot (54).[22] The score's curated randomness emulates the larger message of "contingencies," which Marcos, a paleontologist that Karl interviews in Panama, defines as the "random event(s)" that have produced our present-day realities (10). Contingencies are both random events and actions taken to prepare for said events. Marcos alludes to this second definition as he reminds Karl, accompanied by a jaunty piano vamp, that Panama was "cut in half" to facilitate "global trade and corporations and emissions and populations" because the most important contingency for the world's well-resourced inhabitants is convenience (12).

As scenes crosscut from Karl's experiences and conversations with scientists (studying plants, bugs, bears, and ice) to Phyllis's journey as she follows him, we learn that Karl abandoned his wife and his job as a wildlife reality television director after realizing his complicity in turning the natural world into a media commodity, chronicling but not intervening in species loss. Karl appears in act 1 via a mix of on-stage and live video footage, video chat, and cell phone messages, illustrating the virtual networks of global connection. Although reluctant to become a parent with Phyllis, Karl teams up with and protects the young but worldly activist Julie who leads other young activists in staging their own kidnapping prior to the United Nations climate summit. Their goal: To ransom their return in exchange for meaningful action on climate change by their countries' leaders. Karl serves as a stand-in for artists whose growing awareness of and disillusionment with simply informing about climate change leads them to more direct interventions. Since he meets resistance from his superiors regarding his new "aware" perspective, Karl turns his camera on scientific researchers highlighting the beauty and loss of species (19). Initially, Julie contacts Karl to employ his artistic skills but she later admits her skepticism that visibility alone can have an impact: "I was hoping you'd like draw the realness out of me. Because whatever I've been doing. What we're all doing. It's not enough. I've been on CNN like nine times" (17). As she conceives the self-kidnapping plan, Julie taps into Karl's sense of futility and argues change is only possible by giving up something tangible, something that changes your life: "The message has to be tied to an action. An action that makes it real—this story is about *you.* It's about what you love. And if you do nothing then you, you personally, you have something to lose" (39).

For many of the scientists Phyllis and Karl meet in Panama and Canada, a catastrophic future is by no means already written. In fact, one describes the modeling he does as a way to rehearse different scenarios and see what decisions lead to what outcomes:

> MEDVEDKOV: We present not just one model. It is all the world's models synthesized together. So there is a consensus from our side. From science. But this is the thing. There is the science at one end but at the other there is society. And society makes the policy… . This picture it's one scenario. We run the model using a few different possible futures. Different economic forecasts. Different policy decisions. You see it all comes back to us. Everything we do right now. (72, 73)

The activists and the local inhabitants of these "last of" places where tourists and scientists flock offer less optimism about models and decisions as they know firsthand the previously chosen actions of governments and individuals. Churchill Island offers a northernmost point for an array of climate impacts similar to those on Panama's Barro Colorado Island. Churchill also provides an example of environmental racism in the form of the mid-1950s forced relocation of the nomadic Sayisi Dene tribe from areas in northern Manitoba, Canada where they lived for thousands of years. Almost half of the relocated population died in Churchill without their centuries of land-based traditions and under a segregated existence of poverty and abuse motivated not by the caribou conservation needs stated at the time but by corporate interests and structural racism. Only those who left the resettlement and reconnected with traditional ways were slowly able to rebuild their health and their community:

CHARLIE: So the kids and the survivors they went back where they came from and they saved themselves. So yeah it was awful, but it's not depressing. Cause these people, the ones who survived, they put their world back together. They did it themselves.

(80–81)

Cosson and Friedman only scratch the surface of this genocide but use this notion of building a new world to spur Karl and the young activists on to their unknown journey within the belly of *The Great Immensity*, whose refrain "And the world is wide / And the world is so small" overlaps with Julie's chronicle of small creatures and habitats that are slipping away (86).

The penultimate scene finds Phyllis at a press conference, explaining what has happened: Karl and the "Earth Ambassadors" have left society and they might return "if the agreement happens at Paris. If it gets enforced. If the world changes its course. If we do all that we can to put the world back together. If. If. If. That's the idea. What if?" (84). We then see Julie's final video message to her family explaining how the group will stay away to make the pain of loss more concrete since other absences, extinctions, and catastrophes have not produced sufficient action: "Then maybe everything we've been showing you the past few months. Maybe you'll see it differently" (88). The play's final moment finds Karl, somewhere adrift with his young charges, picking up the ship's refrain about the scale of what we face, wondering whether humans can make the difficult choices needed for their survival, because the more-than-human world does not need us as much as we need it: "For the next fifty years / for the next hundred years / for the next forever without us / the world will still go / the bacteria will thrive / and the grass will still grow" (89).

Big Bigness

Knowing the immensity of their undertaking, Cosson and Friedman shape the audience's experience with an array of theatrical tools. Their characters engage scientific concepts, such as extinction, contingency, ecosystem, resilience, within two interrelated plotlines. The first finds a married couple in conflict over becoming parents as one partner sees in detail how human and more-than-human systems are on the verge of collapse and the other prefers to hope for the best. The second centers on young people, also keenly aware of the lack of time to wait and see, who sever ties with home and family, hoping this action will produce change. Despite the conservative media's pronouncement of the "failure" of a "climate change musical,"[23] theater reviewers for the New York production praised key aspects of the production (e.g., the acting, music, scenography, faithfulness to climate science research). There were no raves but nothing out of step with The Civilians' other new work in its early stages. A unique outcome to the show's run was a "review cluster" published in the winter 2014 issue of *Resilience: A Journal of the Environmental Humanities.* Three scholars reviewed the script and production as "an incunabulum, a work that stands at the beginning of ecotheater's attempts to dramatize climate change."[24] In his essay, Julliard professor of English Anthony Lioi speaks specifically about the play's fragmented takeaways that resist coherence and comfort: "It is a performance of scientific and existential truth that can propagate through the audience in pits of recounted dialogue, fragments of a melody hummed on the way home" ("After the Beautiful Sorrow" 142). All three writers lauded the work for its introspection about the difficulties of storytelling when facing a complex and polarizing issue and trying to reach American audiences where direct impacts of climate change seem far removed from everyday life. And yet, every day that passes illustrates just how much these fantastical and faraway circumstances and catastrophes are no longer fantastical or far away. In the November 2021 issue of the academic journal *Climate and Development*, a trio of respected climate scientists called for an action similar to that of Julie and the Earth Ambassadors: Walk away.[25] They proposed halting climate research until governments and corporations take meaningful action on findings already shared. The response to their proposal has been as divided as broader public opinion on climate change. One member of the Intergovernmental Panel on Climate Change offered a rebuttal that information gathering should continue, but its target audience should be "ordinary people" who are "hungry to know about the changes they are seeing in water supplies, crop yields and fishing patterns" (Zhong).

Trans.Script

Another work in progress that belongs firmly in the realm of the postdramatic is *Frozen Fluid* by Fly Jamerson. The script presents an intriguing interdependence across behavioral, environmental, and physical sciences through the stories of three oceanographers – one a specialist in phytoplankton (Tay), one in glacial melt (Herman), and one in marine mammals (Terra) – who meet, work, and struggle to communicate at a research station in a "mythic Antarctica" during a climate apocalypse. The script, a semifinalist for the O'Neill Festival, has been presented multiple times since 2020 in staged and virtual readings, including a video "accompaniment" with voice-overs produced by the Scoundrel and Scamp Theater for the virtual National Women's Theater Festival Fringe series in July 2021. I base my analysis on this production and all quotations are taken from it.

On their New Play Exchange page, Jamerson describes *Frozen Fluid* as a "series of fables,"[26] and in one interpretation, the play could be set entirely inside the mind of the transgender nonconforming (TGNC) Tay who splits their consciousness into parts – Herman (masc), Terra (femme), and Tay (both/neither) – as they come to know themselves outside of other people's definitions and naming.[27] In another reading, it is a meditation on the ways in which a Christian interpretation of the creation myth, one focused on dominion and possession, fuels both a repressive gender binary and the planet's increasingly catastrophic events. Such forces merge uncomfortably in the scientist characters' navigation of identity and information as the end of the world as we know it seems ever more likely.[28]

Stage directions and scenes without dialogue or with dialogue that repeats in different contexts contain abundant imagery from the Christian Bible (particularly the books of Genesis and Jonah), blurring the lines between climate change and the changes that accompany gender-affirming care.[29] In this world, binaries (man/woman, ice/fire, dead/alive, interior/exterior, end/beginning) are upended when they meet the complexity of human experience. Whether framed in vocabulary from life science, physical science, or behavioral science, such "binaries" are wholly incomplete without a third term. Terra and Tay recall different versions of the creation story from Genesis, the Talmud, and Plato's *Symposium*, finding two of these provide for outcomes beyond man and woman, beyond woman made from man, away from hierarchy toward communion.

We hear more than we see Tay, who narrates their feelings alongside the actions of others. In one scene, Herman and Terra inhabit situations that echo different Bible stories. Herman builds a boat/ark. Terra sits in the belly of a whale, "playing" pregnant by folding a dress and placing it under her shirt. During this, Tay's voice is heard:

> From liquid to solid. It takes time but it seems easier.
> It's what happens when you don't move. When you sit still.
> It takes so much energy to change states the other way.
> From solid to liquid. From frozen to fluid.
> And even if I get there.

If I get there.
It's so fucking cold.

(scene 23)

When all three characters appear together, the physical setting often cracks, melts, slides from under them, emulating relationships hastily built on assumptions and misinterpretations. They share one location as shelter, restroom, and dressing room, and in it, they negotiate physical revelations of bodies and corresponding assumed gender. Is "Tay" actually named "Tay," or is that Terra's and Herman's mishearing their response, "They!" to the question, "What should we call you?" spoken over the howling winds of the Antarctic (scenes 24, 29). Terra reveals she has not corrected her Sunday school students, with whom she exchanges video lessons and correspondence, about Tay not being a man, not realizing she has also misgendered them as a woman (scene 8).

Herman tells Tay the story of his own name being misunderstood (as Vernon[30]) by an expedition engineer speaking and listening through layers of a balaclava and the omnipresent winds. When Herman makes his correction, this individual is shocked and angry: "He looks at me as if he's never seen me." His advice to Tay is to correct Terra's error "before she doesn't know you" (scene 10). Four scenes later, Herman admits that his given name *is* Vernon; he has been going by Herman because "that's who I wanted to be." When Herman tells Terra of his duplicity, he tries to mollify her anger, explaining, "It's just my name. Not who I am" (scene 14). The consequences of naming before knowing move between the human and more-than-human worlds. The scientists' arrival in this place at this time seems motivated by chronicling and charting. "Why did you come here," Tay asks Herman, "if you knew you can't save them [the whales]?" "I just wanna watch," Herman replies. "To watch them. To be here. Maybe by being here something will happen" (scene 10). Such contemplation seems foolhardy given the extreme circumstances, and yet to change the world we have takes time, prioritizing experience over assumption, conservation over faith in never-ending resources. Navigating gender identity, by those outside the direct experience, requires a similar recalibration of expectations, previous narratives, and a nuanced reading of cause, effect, affect, and being. Knowing before naming.

"An Unfathomable Storm"[31]

Frozen Fluid offers a glimpse into what is possible if we reverse course now. If the planet is a metaphor for the psyche of TGNC individuals, both are experiencing catastrophic injury and loss. When faced with a bag of children's letters that request they answer, "Are you a boy or a girl?" by checking "One. Both. Neither," Tay reviews their options of being who they are when they are alone and when they are with others:

> I feel more comfortable in my body than I ever have before.
> I feel balanced, and healthy, and at peace.
> I feel acceptance and awe at this complex, resilient, squishy machine.
> But.
> I have a heightened awareness of my body in space.
> Of how people talk about me. To me.
> Of how people look at my body.
> Of how people talk about me, to me, after they look at my body.
> That's when I feel uncomfortable.
>
> (scene 11)

There is a certain amount of unknowing, dispossession that accompanies this state of being. To name, dominate, and multiply is such a pervasive national mythology. Taxonomies are a key indexical prop of both the sciences and the arts. "To identify" comes with an attachment of certain social values to supposedly "natural" or scientific principles that are themselves constructions. Tay does not offer a biology lesson to debunk the gender binary; instead, they articulate identity as states of matter to illuminate how they navigate a troubled world.

Shining a spotlight on humanity's destructive behavior is something theater does particularly well, as Chandhuri notes:

> By making space on its stage for ongoing acknowledgments of the rupture it participates in – the rupture between nature and culture, forests and books, sincere acting and real fish – the theater can become the site of a much-needed ecological consciousness.
>
> (28)

Frozen Fluid reminds us that healing one set of attitudes and perceptions across art and science is only one part of a larger, connected web of knowledge and behaviors. It is a risky proposition to connect, even metaphorically, the complexities of environmental science to human identity; however, *Frozen Fluid* might come the closest to fulfilling the promise of a dramaturgy of interdependence: connecting our understanding of human identity to environmental change. Many science plays, even those that explore the multiverses of theoretical physics, present a world where human form, action, and contemplation dominate. Environmentally oriented work, such as that discussed here, helps shift our perspectives from human-only to human-among-the-more-than-human without succumbing to despair about the magnitude of intertwined issues or cavalierly dismissing the immediacy of threats because the worst has not befallen us yet.

Notes

1 This is a paraphrase of the opening sentence of Caridad Svich's essay "On Unmaking Theater in *Theatre: A Love Story.*"

2 See Christensen for the differences between global warming and climate change.

3 This language is a nod to Donna Haraway's 2016 *Staying with the Trouble: Making Kin in the Chthulucene* (Duke University Press).

4 See May and Fried.

5 Within this quote, Brown cites his own writing on the development process of his play *Half a Life* about the impact of 1960s-era nuclear testing on veterans who served in the Maralinga area of South Australia, their families, and the local community.

6 See the award-winning reporting of Bruce Nolan and other staff writers at the *Times Picayune* for a chronicle of the immediate and long-term aftermath of Hurricane Katrina.

7 According to NOAA's 2013 "Tropical Cyclone Report" for Sandy, costs to New York alone were estimated to be $19 billion of a total cost of $70 billion to all regions affected along the southeast and northeast coast.

8 Works on Water has become a nonprofit organization and triennial exhibition. Read more at www.worksonwater.org/what-we-do.

9 The script operates with the expectation that subjecting audiences to a simulated emergency evacuation will be manageable for a production.

10 Tess Mayer's photo essay in the June 2017 issue of *The Interval* chronicles how installations from Paloma MacGregor ("Building a Better Fishtrap"), Marina Zurkow ("Floating Studio for Dark Ecologies"), and the art collective Mare Liberum ("A Decade Platform") comprised the scenic landscape of the *(Not) Water* 2017 production.

11 The script also contains a section of part 3, titled *Remedy Valley Centennial Pageant* and written by Liza Birkenmeier that was not staged at 3LD.

12 The script indicates the character of THE SCIENTIST "grabs" people from the larger crowd and pulls them into the bathroom. From my recollection of the June 25, 2017 performance, the audience could choose to meet either THE SCIENTIST or THE COOK.

13 Works on Water has an impressive commission history for site-specific work, but so far, the entity has not produced a printed collection.

14 Read more at the website for the Smithsonian Tropical Research Institute at Barro Colorado, Columbia, stri.si.edu/facility/barro-colorado.

15 Read more at the website for the Northern Studies Centre in Churchill, Canada, churchillscience.ca/.
16 Imagining The Civilians' $697,177 grant was distributed over the course of three fiscal years (2010–13 with reporting completed in summer 2014), an average of $230,000 per year remains an impressive amount. According to the National Endowment for the Art's (NEA's) press release for 2021, the average NEA grant to individual organizations is about $25,000 even for multiyear projects.
17 The summary abstract for the NSF grant award #1010974 is archived at www.informalscience.org/great-immensity.
18 I have not been able to access TheGreatImmensity.org from its original URL since 2019.
19 A July 2013 casting call in *Backstage* still indicated the Polly/Phyllis double-casting of one actor to play the identical twins.
20 The 2015 United Nations Climate Change Conference (COP21) produced the "Paris Agreement," from which the United States withdrew in 2017. The character of Julie could have been based on activist Greta Thunberg, who began the School Strike for Climate action in August 2018 except for the fact Julie predates Thunberg's appearance on the world stage.
21 Lyric quotations and music descriptions are informed by the script draft as well as *The Great Immensity* soundtrack released in 2019 as part of *The Michael Friedman Collection*.
22 In interviews about the play's title (see Trussell), Cosson and Friedman cited their own experience on a Panama Canal boat that ferried tourists being passed by a cargo ship that almost capsized their small craft. The hull bore the Chinese characters that roughly translated to "The Great Immensity."
23 See Moti and Miller as two options, among many, with language that comes to infuse conservative pundit talking points from 2013 onward. These sources include specific criticism for government funding of the arts as a collaborative partner with science and discuss the kind of science that the writers claim deserves funding.
24 In his introduction to the review cluster, Lioi cites The Civilians' Next Forever Initiative to develop new work employing an ecodramaturgy that is responsive to the current crisis. After Friedman's untimely death in 2017 and the COVID-19 pandemic's impact on theatrical production in the United States, it is unclear where this initiative currently stands.
25 Glavovic and his coauthors offer different options to prompt action; a "strike" is the "more radical" option, but they argue it is the "only effective way to arrest the tragedy of climate change science" (4).
26 Jamerson's recent work list on their New Play Exchange profile page includes a host of ecodrama commissions. They also count Lauren Gunderson as a key mentor to their work.
27 Current casting notes request TGNC actors for all characters so that the entire trio reflects the "fluid" of the title.
28 About two-thirds through the play, there are clues that the world actually ends. Stage directions read: *The Earth stops turning. The wind picks up rapidly. An unfathomable storm* (*Frozen Fluid*, scene 20).
29 Transition may or may not include surgery. Jamerson seems to imagine medical intervention in moments where characters are pierced in the

stomach and struggle over whether they should harpoon beached whales to end their suffering.

30 Like Herman/Vernon, Terra/Tara and Tay/They are all possibly misunderstood names that shift when spoken/heard versus written/read.

31 Language from the stage directions in scene 20.

References

Arons, Wendy, and Theresa J. May. *Readings in Performance and Ecology.* Palgrave Macmillan, 2012.

Bianchi, Chris. "Hurricane Katrina: 15 Years Later." *Spectrum News Tampa Bay News 9*, 30 Aug. 2020. www.baynews9.com/fl/tampa/weather/2020/08/29/hurricane-katrina-15-years-later.

Blake, Eric S., et al. "Tropical Cyclone Report: Hurricane Sandy 22–29 October 2012." National Hurricane Center, National Oceanic and Atmospheric Administration, 12 Feb. 2013. nhc.noaa.gov/data/tcr/AL182012_Sandy.pdf.

Brown, Paul. "Ecological Knowledge in Community Theater." *CLCWeb: Comparative Literature and Culture*, vol. 16, no. 4, 2001. doi:10.7771/1481-4374.2584.

Brown, Paul, editor. *Verbatim: Staging Memory & Community.* Currency, 2010.

Brown, Paul, and Xanthe Crittenden. "Nature Moves Centre Stage: Eco-centrism in Community Theater." *About Performance*, vol. 7, 2007, pp. 99–116. https://www.proquest.com/scholarly-journals/nature-moves-centre-stage-eco-centrism-community/docview/1710647967/se-2?accountid=10598.

Callaghan, Sheila. *(Not) Water.* Unpublished manuscript. Courtesy of the author.

Chaudhuri, Una. "'There Must Be a Lot of Fish in That Lake': Toward an Ecological Theater." *Theater*, vol. 25, no. 1, 1994, pp. 23–31.

Christensen, Jen. "Is It Climate Change or Global Warming? How Science and a Secret Memo Shaped the Answer." *CNN*, 2 Mar. 2019. cnn.com/2019/03/02/world/global-warming-climate-change-language-scn/index.html.

Collins-Hughes, Laura. "A Play on Water, Made Drop by Drop." *New York Times*, 11 June 2017. https://www.proquest.com/newspapers/play-on-water-made-drop/docview/1908008680/se-2?accountid=10598.

Cosson, Steve, and Michael Friedman. *The Great Immensity.* Unpublished manuscript. 2015. newplayexchange.org/users/27924/steve-cosson.

Friedman, Michael. "Cabaret as Drama (with Apologies to Joseph Kerman)." *Contemporary Theatre Review*, vol. 16, no. 3, 2006, pp. 318–326. doi:10.1080/10486800600817345.

Friedman, Michael. *The Great Immensity* (Soundtrack). The Civilians World Premiere Recording. *The Michael Friedman Collection*. Ghostlight Records. 2019. iTunes.

Gibbons, Sarah. "Hurricane Sandy: Explained." *National Geographic.com*, 11 Feb. 2019. nationalgeographic.com/environment/article/hurricane-sandy.

Glavovic, Bruce, Timothy F. Smith, and Iain White. "The Tragedy of Climate Change Science." *Climate and Development*, 2021, pp. 1–5. doi:10.1080/17565529.2021. 2008855.

GreatImmensity.org. *Internet Archive*, web.archive.org/web/20140402165815/http://www.thegreatimmensity.org/.

Guthrie, Adrian John. "*When the Way Out Was In: Avant-garde Theater in Australia, 1965–1985*." 1996. University of Wollongong, PhD thesis. ro.uow.edu.au/theses/1762.

Jamerson, Tay. Author page for "Frozen Fluid." *New Play Exchange*. newplayexchange.org/plays/371459/frozen-fluid.

Jamerson, Tay. *Frozen Fluid*. 17 Jul. 2021 online performance for the Women's Theatre Festival (NC). Streamed and archived on YouTube. youtu.be/76OihDvbiAo.

Lioi, Anthony. "After the Beautiful Sorrow: Affective Resilience and *The Great Immensity*." *Resilience: A Journal of the Environmental Humanities*, vol. 2, no. 1, 2015, pp. 140–144. doi:10.5250/resilience.2.1.009.

Lioi, Anthony. "Introduction to *The Great Immensity*." *Resilience: A Journal of the Environmental Humanities*, vol. 2, no. 1, 2015, pp. 113–114. doi:10.5250.resilience.2.1.014.

Loop News. "Five Most Destructive Hurricanes of the Last Decade." *Carribean.LoopNews.com*, 20 Jul. 2020. caribbean.loopnews.com/content/five-most-destructive-hurricanes-last-decade.

May, Theresa J. *Earth Matters on Stage: Ecology and Environment in American Theater*. Routledge, 2020.

May, Theresa J., and Larry Fried. *Greening Up Our Houses: A Guide to an Ecologically Sound Theatre*. Drama Book Publishers, 1994.

Mayer, Tess. "Photo Essay: Behind the Scenes of (Not) Water." *The Interval.com*, 15 June 2017. theintervalny.com/featurettes/2017/06/photo-essay-behind-the-scenes-of-not-water/.

Miller, Henry I. "$697,177 for a 'Climate-Change Musical': You Call That Science?" *Wall Street Journal*, 13 May 2017. https://www.proquest.com/newspapers/697-177-climate-change-musical-you-call-that/docview/1898370422/se-2.

Moti, Luboš. "*The Great Immensity:* NSF-Funded AGW Theater Play." 30 Mar. 2014. motls.blogspot.com/2014/03/the-great-immensity-nsf-funded-agw.html.

"National Endowment for the Arts Supports the Arts with over $27.5 Million in Awards in First Round of FY2021 Funding." National Endowment for the Arts, 4 Feb. 2021. arts.gov/about/news/2021/national-endowment-arts-supports-arts-over-275-million-awards-first-round-fy2021-funding.

National Hurricane Center. "Hurricane Katrina Advisory Archive. August 23–30, 2005." National Oceanic and Atmospheric Administration. nhc.noaa.gov/archive/2005/KATRINA.shtml.

Nolan, Bruce. "CATASTROPHIC. Storm Surge Swamps 9th Ward, St. Bernard Lakeview Levee Breach Threatens to Inundate City." *The Times-Picayune* (New Orleans, LA), 30 Aug. 2005, A1–2.

Odendahl-James, Jules. Instructor Notes. *Performing Science*, Duke University, 23 Mar. 2011.

Peters, Carol. "Q&A: The Making of The Great Immensity." High Meadows Environmental Institute Princeton University, 15 May 2010, environment.princeton.edu/news/qa-the-making-of-the-great-immensity/.

Radosavljević, Duška, et al. "Caridad Svich & Pedro de Senna - Rumble Dramaturgies." *LMYE [Lend Me Your Ears] Salon #3. Auralia.Space*, 2021. Royal Central School of Speech and Drama, doi:10.25389/rcssd.14015357.v2.

Shepherd-Barr, Kirsten. *Science on Stage: From Doctor Faustus to Copenhagen*. Princeton University Press, 2006.

Shepherd-Barr, Kirsten. *Theatre and Evolution from Ibsen to Beckett*. Columbia University Press, 2015.

Soloski, Alexis. "Review: '(Not) Water' Offers Too Much to Drink In." *New York Times*, 19 June 2017, https://www.proquest.com/newspapers/review-not-water-offers-too-much-drink/docview/1910709460/se-2?accountid=10598.

Svich, Caridad. "On Unmaking Theater in *Theatre: A Love Story*." *Theater*, vol. 51, no. 3, 2021, pp. 57–59. doi:10.1215/01610775-9402453.

"The Civilians' The Great Immensity [Casting Call]." *Back Stage East*, vol. 54, no. 29, 18 July 2013, p. 30. link.gale.com/apps/doc/A339119518/ITOF?u=duke_perkins&sid=bookmark-ITOF&xid=2c0ed5d2.

Tran, Diep. "Tech + Text." *American Theatre*, vol. 3, no. 6, 2016, pp. 18–24. https://www.proquest.com/trade-journals/tech-text/docview/1803678869/se-2?accountid=10598.

Trussell, Robert. "Amusing Encounter Led to The Great Immensity a Play about Global Warming." *Kansas City Star* [MO], 17 Feb. 2012. infoweb.newsbank.com/apps/news/document-view?p=AMNEWS&docref=news/13CFA1F827DB5E80.

Zehelein, Eva-Sabine. *Science: Dramatic. Science Plays in America and Great Britain, 1990–2007*. Universitätsverlag Winter, 2009.

Zhong, Raymond. "These Climate Scientists Are Fed Up and Ready to Go on Strike." *New York Times*, 1 Mar. 2022. nytimes.com/2022/03/01/climate/ipcc-climate-scientists-strike.html.

Zinoman, Jason. "The Curtain Rises: Enter, Reality: When News Events Are Retold Onstage." *New York Times*, 8 Dec. 2010, p. C1.

3 Dramaturgy of Participation

Citizen Science: A Brief Primer

In the late-nineteenth century, U.S. researchers in the fields of ornithology and meteorology invited public contributions to their scientific data collection, building on the hobbies of bird-watching and the traditions of the *Farmer's Almanac* to gather observational evidence from locations far beyond the emerging lab spaces of universities and institutes.[1] Almost 100 years later, Rick Bonney, first a volunteer, then director of education at the Cornell Lab of Ornithology (CLO), used the term "citizen science" in a successful 1993 National Science Foundation (NSF) grant to support the lab's national science experiments (NSEs) "intended to involve the public in a series of guided projects in which participants would gather information desired by ornithologists, while, at the same time, learning more about birds and about how scientific projects are conducted" (Trunbull et al. 266). Bonney continued to employ the term in public communications, as CLO became a hub for such projects and its researchers began to organize and assess both public participation and resulting data with greater scrutiny. Working simultaneously but not collaboratively, Danish sociologist Alan Irwin explored the term's parameters for use in public policy and science and technology studies. In his 1995 book, *Citizen Science: A Study of People, Expertise, and Sustainable Development*, Irwin provides a nuanced examination of the concept's central dynamics between the general public and scientists who often interact in the crucible of regulation over products and practices: "For scientists and social scientists alike, the contexts within which expertise becomes applied within everyday life are important sites of reflection and discovery" (xi). For Irwin, the boundaries of expertise gain significance as scientific professionalism has shaped knowledge held by "ordinary citizens" since the Industrial Revolution and individuals

DOI: 10.4324/9781003150848-4

encounter scientific developments through education, work, everyday life habits, or transformative events (10–11).

Irwin offers two definitions for citizen science. First, it is "science which assists the needs and concerns of citizens," a broad arena that can include advancements employed by industries (from petrochemical to pharmaceutical to technological) and results in products for purchase and in systems that can be protested if they imperil a location or way of life (3–4). The second meaning encompasses forms "of science [and scientific knowledge] developed and enacted by the citizens themselves" (4). Irwin notes how a lack of social equity can stifle the collaborative spirit between citizens and scientific experts perceived to work for systems that threaten the public's survival: "Science is the servant of power – its investigations claim to open the possibilities for policy making but instead serve to reinforce the existing social order" (30). His Europe-based case studies depict opportunities where "the public" and "science" are drawn closer together in collaborations marked by democratically oriented, productive disruptions of hierarchical knowledge structures enforced by governments, corporations, and even academia (2). American citizen science scholars Caren Cooper and Bruce Lewenstein also notice how often these collaborations center on "environmental monitoring and environmental justice," where "practitioners and participants seek to transform the power dynamics of local, regional, national and even international communities" (59). Irwin argues these informal and cocreated science learning opportunities can provide "self-critical and self-aware forms of knowledge and understanding," empowering individuals with new "ways of knowing and acting" (175) a kind of "environmental citizenship" that offers a "meeting point for a number of current dichotomies": social/natural, local/global, personal/public, technical/informal (178, 180).

Over time, the citizen science mission that CLO began has expanded beyond projects where broad swath of volunteers participate in informal scientific education through highly structured research practices that are evaluated and acted on by scientific professionals. For Cooper and Lewenstein, current best practices within scientific fields promote collaborations that emulate democratic function, debate, and broad inclusion (59). Various taxonomies have emerged to identify this rapidly expanding terrain. Geographer Muki Haklay emphasizes that such classificatory structures should avoid judgment or hierarchy and include endeavors where outcomes challenge assumptions and authority. He organizes citizen science work into participatory levels from 1, projects dependent on the largest numbers and broadest array of volunteers, to 4, projects that are fully collaborative across amateurs, students, and experts who cocreate research questions, data collection, analysis, and communication post project ("Citizen Science" 115–119).[2] The goal is not to codify citizen science projects into one ideal. Instead, Haklay emphasizes any structure should be based on project outcomes and the best tools and ethics to offer inclusion and engagement to all involved ("Participatory Citizen Science" 54).

Citizen Science Art

Haklay describes citizen science projects that tackle seeming intractable and complex social problems as encountering uncertainty that complicates definitive action and conclusions. The collaborative research within a citizen science process provides all participants, including scientific experts, with "capacity building" for difficult decisions ("Participatory Citizen Science" 54). In this way, contemporary citizen science projects invite a **dramaturgy of participation** as scientists work with a variety of untrained individuals navigating ongoing impacts of large-scale events or unique occurrences by recording, assessing, representing, and communicating their findings. Instead of turning a dramaturgical lens onto citizen science projects (something Irwin's book does admirably, though without any direct invocation of dramaturgy), this chapter focuses on theater projects where the dynamics of community participation within artistic research and its communication are similarly complex: *SPILL* by writer/director Leigh Fondakowski, *Ocean Filibuster* by the avant-garde duo PearlDamour, and *Rollover* by climate geologist Laura J. Moore. These works do not fall neatly under documentary or ethnodrama performance categories though they possess some of those features in the way artists, community members, and scientific researchers function as cocreators (though not always credited officially). The artists take the lead in transforming quantitative and qualitative research into theatrical language, sometimes as realistic testimony, sometimes as fantastical imaginings, in an effort to illuminate the complexities of community decision-making that includes scientists as uniquely informed members of the citizenry. In *Rollover*, a scientist takes the lead as citizen artist to reconcile the sometimes-contradictory modes of the two cultures' inquiry and assessment practices, offering a theatrical experience as rehearsal for future participatory decision-making.

Currently, these pieces are unpublished and the publication and reproduction of this work can be complicated by the specificity of events surrounding their creation and extended development process, as well as the artists' goals regarding production. The climate concerns at the center of each piece are rendered differently based on participation and collaboration: from disciplinary experts whose experiences and research inspire the text's content, those who contribute information or analysis from lived experience, and those who comprise the script's audience, contributing their spectatorial experiences for assessment. The projects often review and redraft what verbatim theater scholar Paul Brown calls "intractable legacies and injustice," such as environmental racism and extractive economies, "while [also] celebrating expressions of hope and positive actions" ("Ecological Knowledge" 3). The Sloan Foundation and other private entities appear in the funding structures of some of this work; however, these projects sit at a distance the science plays discussed in chapter 1, which prioritize humanity for the scientist and can reinforce science's power and prestige. The artists discussed here often build ties with institutions of higher education. As interdisciplinary, creative research, this work raises questions about credibility and authority since science and art assess impact and rigor with different scales of value and success. While *The Great Immensity* illustrates how artistic work may find a sponsor in the NSF under the "informal science education" category, the decade-plus political fallout of The Civilians' $699,900 award for this show illustrates the complicated metrics of success faced by government-funded interdisciplinary collaboration. The chapter concludes with a discussion of *Rollover*'s pursuit of NSF funding and a brief review of *The Great Immensity*'s NSF evaluation, touching on these complications with particular attention to artistic creation as it meets impact assessment.

The Art of Risk(y) Science

Leigh Fondakowski's *SPILL* harkens to early-twentieth-century theatrical traditions themselves foreshadowing the existential dramaturgy of post–World War II theater. If citizen science can trace some of its U.S. origins to late-nineteenth-century bird and weather watchers, one can draw a similar line between the "citizen theater" represented by *SPILL* to the 1930s Federal Theatre Project (FTP) when artists enjoyed a brief window of inclusion as public workers who received direct government funding for their craft. With theatrical influences from Western Europe and Russia and emerging mass media industries, forms like the Living Newspaper emerged from collaborations including professional artists, pedagogues of early theater training programs, non-arts disciplinary experts, and members of the wider public. In some Living Newspapers, the audience was represented on stage by a range of characters depicting a "social and economic role" instead of internal conflict or psychology – for instance, "the Little Man" who could serve as audience proxy by asking questions and making decisions based on information learned (Highsaw 16). Living Newspapers' subject matter was dominated by the positive transformation of the average American's life through government intervention itself assisted by a growing scientific sector improving housing, access to clean water, electrical power, agricultural regulation, and public health. In a similar way, *SPILL* represents a story of how scientific knowledge can help individuals make informed decisions and a story of how scientific knowledge can impede resistance to risky regulatory or deregulatory actions of governments and industries that prize extraction and consumption. It emulates some theatrical techniques of Living Newspapers: verbatim testimony (from court records and newspapers) blended with nonlinear narrative structures, large casts of mostly one-dimensional characters, expressionistic and modular scenic/staging elements that facilitate multiple locations and chronologies. The play foregrounds human losses in an effort to show communal dependence, a dependence that can deepen our resolve to act toward the greater good while negotiating our self-interests. *SPILL* dramatizes a specific historical event to anticipate the questions that emerge whenever or wherever disaster strikes, requiring communities to examine their choices and even engage in civic actions to hold industries and institutions responsible for theirs.

SPILL did not originate as a Sloan commission; however, it is currently the only interview-based piece recorded by LA Theatre Works for the Sloan-funded *Relativity* series of science-themed plays and Sloan supported Ensemble Studio Theatre's 2017 production of the script.[3] The genesis of *SPILL* was Wesleyan University's Creative Campus Initiative, pairing non-arts faculty with artists for cross-disciplinary work. Environmental science professor Barry Chernoff cotaught a cross-listed theater and environmental studies course with Fondakowski, engaging the interviewing and playmaking techniques she developed as an original member of the Tectonic Theatre Company to inform a fuller understanding of the Deepwater Horizon explosion's aftermath.[4] Speaking to TimeLine Theater artistic director PJ Powers in advance of that company's 2015 production of *SPILL*, Fondakowski explains the early development timeline. Chernoff and Fondakowski's first research trip to the Gulf Coast happened in the fall of 2010 a few months after the active spill had been stopped, when industry and government agencies were releasing their assessments of the disaster and the six-month moratorium on offshore drilling put in place by the Obama administration was coming to an end. When they returned with students in the summer of 2011, the group took a closer look at Louisiana's complicated ecosystem of land, oil and gas industries, and people: 3 million acres of marshes, swamps, forest, and barrier island habitats with a human population of over 2 million living in proximity to 150 active petrochemical plants, over 250 offshore oil drilling platforms and rigs, and a pre-spill commercial fishing industry that provided 1 in every 70 jobs.[5] Using "moment work," a collection of techniques wherein collaborators build characters often from interviews and/or archival materials and build action from an array of objects and images, paying close attention to space and sound (Kaufman et al.), Fondakowski's student team produced an early draft of the script that included conversations with environmental scientists, local commercial fishermen, and industry and government officials. After the class ended, impacts remained from the oil on shores, in estuaries, and from the cleanup measures such as the chemical dispersants that BP sprayed from the air onto the ocean surface. Fondakowski found both the deceased men's family members (themselves often current or former oil rig workers) and south Louisiana community members more willing to talk about their experiences. Between 2011 and 2013, she returned to Louisiana's coast over a dozen times, gathering 200 hours of footage, connecting with a broad range of individuals, and deepening connections with a core set of informants who would become the central characters around which *SPILL* swirls (Wesleyan).

SPILL's Flow

Fondakowski portrays her investigative work within *SPILL* through the character of the Writer/Narrator who, like a Living Newspaper's "Little Man," poses questions and demonstrates active listening with workers, experts, and families (Powers). The audience experiences the multiple modes of communication (journals, letters, phone calls, court testimony) invoked by the playwright's sources. These choices reflect a "show your work" dimension of documentary theater where confirmable, often publicly vetted or witnessed events are shaped into a specific story through edits and elaborations. Scenes that contain or imply interview materials or mechanics lend veracity and authority to the story, its teller, its process, and its private contexts now made public. Such features might be considered akin to the methods section of a citizen science project research paper. In *SPILL*, we follow the network of referrals interviewees entrust to the Writer. Such structure indicates a chain of lived experience and reinforces the idea that the playwright ethically conveys participants' situational or professional expertise and their stories. In the previously mentioned TimeLine interview, Fondakowski tells Powers,

> The community is the protagonist. The playwriting process is also about letting many voices speak and become part of the greater story being told… . We tried to find communities that had not been represented in the media, communities that were "off the map," so to speak.

The rig workers themselves represent types of citizen scientists as *SPILL* shows us the range of education, research, and authority they possess. Highly advanced technology and years of testing and development go into the high-risk venture of deepwater oil drilling, a process akin to space flight in its limited capacity to test for all possible scenarios and to require a variety of expertise for day-to-day operations (from entirely manual labor on-site to lab-based mathematical modeling). Such disparity illuminates not just a divide of scientific and engineering knowledge between the petroleum industry and the general public but within the industry itself. *SPILL* raises key questions about the relationship between technical capacities supported by geophysical science, mechanical engineering, financial investment, and the ethical limits on those capacities necessitated by potential and active harms to people, places, and the public good.

Part 1 establishes the Writer/Narrator as community outsider on a journey to reconstruct a rough timeline of events with the blowout and workers' casualties comprising the climatic event. She gives deceased rig worker Jason Anderson the most complete character arc. In him, she finds a synecdoche for thousands of workers who earn their living connected in some way to the many tendrils of the petroleum industry. Bob Bea, expert witness and former rig engineer, describes Anderson's career trajectory made possible by drilling:

> BEA: The American dream is still alive and kicking in the oil and gas industry. One of the few places left where a guy can start out as a roughneck, work his way up to a rig manager, and then all the way to the top. A VIP. $200,000 a year with only two years of college… . Here, this is Jason Anderson, thirty-four-year-old toolpusher. That's where he was headed. Top management. A talented man.
>
> (*SPILL*, part 1, 14.00–14.30)

Anderson was a son, husband, father, and worker who learned much of his expertise on the job. We hear of his deep investment in the company that employed him and learn he kept his own record of the times his warnings about drilling pace were dismissed. *SPILL*'s part 2 tracks three concurrent lines of action: (1) the desperate drive to stop the oil flow, (2) the cleanup efforts to protect the coastline, and (3) the specter of government regulation and industry next steps. The dead's loved ones disagree with even a brief drilling moratorium, revealing the region's economic dependence on petroleum. Commercial fishers describe their willingness to participate in dangerously unsupervised cleanup efforts, not just to protect the coastal wetlands but because these cleanup jobs paid well. Anderson's ghost serves as a counterpoint to the living but forever-changed Gulf fisher Jory Danos, a member of BP's "Citizen's Army," recruited as part of their "vessels of opportunity" program ("Factsheet") to supplement the use of chemical dispersant spray to keep the leaking oil away from the shoreline. Danos leaped at BP's allowances of up to $300/day and calls to "come be a hero … be a part of history." As his anger grows in telling about how little protection the company provided – "We had no respirators. No training. Tyvek suits and gloves. That's it" – it is met by self-directed fury at sacrificing his future health for immediate money (*SPILL* part 2, 30.00–34.00).

In part 2, while the "spill cam" projects the oil flow over the steel rigging and metal table surfaces of *SPILL*'s set, a range of experts (including officials from BP via depositions and trial transcripts) describe how repairing the catastrophe requires another layer of engineering research and experimentation, one being created in real time. Even as they are successful in their efforts to stanch the well, Fondakowski gives Bea, the engineer, a final word to posit that lessons learned from Deepwater might not be enough to prevent the next disaster or the pursuit of even more complex drilling excursions:

BEA: We have now gotten into extraction systems so complex the consequences of failure are so dramatically greater and now we want to go to the Arctic. Are you kidding me? A blowout in winter, under the ice? I've had to confront my colleagues at Shell. They show me all the gizmos. I say, "I know we have gizmos to do it. But should we?"

(*SPILL*, part 2, 41.23–41.45)

Bea's query is echoed by Shelly Anderson, Jason's widow, as she approaches the one-year anniversary of his death: "Could I have done something differently? Should I have seen this coming?" (*SPILL*, part 2, 44.45–44.49). Her questions are for everyone. What can we do individually, collectively to change our relationship with oil, with the environment, with each other? What should we do, and to whom should we look for guidance?

Echoing Tectonic's decision to stage the first full production of *The Laramie Project* in Laramie, *SPILL*'s April 2014 world premiere was at the Swine Palace Theatre in Baton Rouge, Louisiana (Giola). At intermission, full-size portraits of key characters painted by Reeva Wortel, a visual artist who accompanied Fondakowski on interviews, graced the theater lobby. Community members were represented on stage by professional actors (Troeh). The premiere within its characters' city/state, however, prioritizes their presence as a key measure of the work's success. When she delivered an address at Wesleyan University six months later, Fondakowski described a largely positive reception, affirming her commitment to the deep listening and community participation embedded in her process. Even though *SPILL* has not yet forged the same rallying cry that surrounded *The Laramie Project*, Fondakowski spoke of the production in Baton Rouge as filled with potential. By focusing on the workers as citizens most directly dependent on and deeply invested in the status quo, Fondakowski asserted the artist's responsibility to transform an echo chamber into a channel for communication:

> We're in this predicament together. In such a polarized political climate, people believe things because of their lived experience. We need to be listening to each other in a different kind of way, not in terms of right or wrong. We're all implicated; we all have to be part of the solution.

SPILL relies on well-tested mechanics of documentary theater to fortify its claims that although there is clear fault for the Deepwater Horizon's rig disaster, the responsibility for what came before and after reverberates far beyond the Gulf Coast. In keeping with its documentary lineage, *SPILL* works diligently to "construct an objective view" of an event "but nevertheless stimulates engagement and identification in the subjective register" (Reinelt 19). The next citizen science art collaboration to be discussed pushes away from negotiated indexical realism, decentering human consciousness, and expanding the concept of citizen to more-than-human actors.

Humans as Central Actors but Not at the Center of the Action

Eco-theater scholar Una Chaudhuri has asked, "Are we human beings and our activities such as theater an integral part of nature, or are we somehow radically separate from it?" (27). The debate among stratigraphers over whether and when the Holocene (the age of humans) becomes the Anthropocene (the age of human effects) poses a similar question using different evidentiary measures to discover the answer (Myer). In theater and representational art that takes up climate change, there is the added complication of how to stress the pivotal roles humans play in environmental impact while also decentering humans as primary characters in the script of planetary life. Additionally, the human point of view is often positioned as a citizen from a well-resourced nation-state. Although the intensity, unpredictability, and ubiquity of catastrophic events has equalized some life-changing experiences for human beings, the recent COVID-19 pandemic has illustrated that shared experiences vary widely across dimensions of local and global difference.

One company navigating these aspects of new work development is PearlDamour. Founders, director Katie Pearl and playwright Lisa D'Amour, add to their company rosters project to project the last three of which – *How to Build a Forest, Milton*, and *Ocean Filibuster* – connect the collaborative dimensions of art making with an embedded commitment to civic life especially around those dimensions rife with interpersonal and interdisciplinary complexity. The company reflects a new iteration of both science play and community-based creative research. Pearl argues in her "We Are the Climate" essay contribution to the 2017 edition of Howlround.com's open-source series "Theater in the Age of Climate Change,"

> The focus can no longer be on impactful storytelling. We can't stop there because those stories aren't reaching enough people. We can't stop there because our current metrics of success, including getting reviewed in major publications, keep us from heading towards different kinds of performance work that might have a different kind of impact, and affect more change. We can't stop there because as theatre artists, our power doesn't merely exist in the plays we create and the stories we tell. It also exists in our creativity itself.

Pearl's vision of a citizen artist echoes that of Michael Rohd's *Howl-Round* call for "art making as civic practice," encouraging theater makers to consider collaborative, public action as new work. Like Rohd, PearlDamour initiates projects that take place within theater spaces but both build their work out of a range of non-arts partnerships touching on scientific research, economic analysis, and public policy.

From *Forest* to *Ocean Filibuster*

Previously, I have written about the company's *How to Build a Forest* residency at Duke University in 2012, describing the piece as one that "embeds a logic of connectivity between the natural world and human effects on the environment" within a "decidedly artificial ecosystem" (Odendahl-James 384). It took 12 months of planning, curriculum building, grant writing, and sponsorship wrangling to bring *Forest* to campus for three free performances and a live-stream video. Such extensive preparation and integration reflect a development and production format that exceeds the infrastructure of most commercial theaters in the United States. For *Milton*, PearlDamour bypassed regional theaters, working instead within rural communities similar to the traditions of other companies such as Cornerstone (Los Angeles), Sojourn (Portland, then Chicago, now Tempe), and Ten Thousand Things (Twin Cities). The central product in *Milton* was an event performed by professional artists; however, it was built from and alongside a series of interconnected though not simultaneous community engagements in five towns across the United States named Milton (in Massachusetts, North Carolina, Louisiana, Oregon, and Wisconsin). Although *Milton*'s subject is not climate change, in its creation PearlDamour models an approach to collaboration that recognizes similar stakes in building a community. Because the impacts are varied, opinions heated, depth of information scarce, and strategies difficult to implement as they often involve change and compromise, the idea of finding consensus, navigating shared and separate histories, and negotiating dialogue are parts of theater making that can play critical roles in crafting a shared future. In a 2020 interview with *Wesleyan University Magazine* managing editor Himeka Curiel, Pearl argues that theater needs to evolve its definitions of "actor," "audience," and "production" to include all who participate in "a community that is using the creative moment to come together, to address a question, to investigate a shared experience, to dream, and to challenge [a] situation."

PearlDamour's inspiration for *Milton* stemmed from a desire to shift perspective away from the bubble of urban arts enclaves when seeking answers to fundamental questions about **existence** (Why do you think we're on this earth?), **inheritance** (What is your advice to future generations?), **identity** (How did you get to this town?), and **influence** (If you could change one thing about the world, what would it be?) (D'Amour, Pearl, and Kremer 85).[6] Since it is devised work, the expansiveness of source materials, particularly each town's citizens, meant that creative roles and responsibilities were flexible, and outcomes beyond the central play's performance could be as varied as a street fair, murals, and other visual arts installations. The "Skies over Milton" photo series and artist Jim Findlay's video projections are nods to the way air and sky connect and divide these places. They also comprise the key scenic elements that link the performances presented in five very different venues.[7]

Around the time *Milton* was wrapping its culminating performances, Harvard's American Repertory Theatre and Center for the Environment (HUCE) commissioned PearlDamour to create what has become *Ocean Filibuster.* D'Amour described an early conversation with Peter Girguis, professor of organismic and evolutionary biology, recounting his first journey in a submersible to the ocean floor: "His first thought was 'community.' All these things living in community."[8] This term connected PearlDamour's creative aesthetic, the scientists' lab work and research, and the imagined goal for the commission: To inspire understanding of the daunting, shared work humans face around climate change. Similar to The Civilians' work at Princeton's Environmental Institute that produced *The Great Immensity*, PearlDamour had autonomy over the resulting product. While in conversation at HUCE, the artists quickly homed in on the "wonder" that environmental scientists felt about their work. Individual research projects contribute to the landscape of *Ocean*, but there are no scientist characters. Scientific information is embodied within the performance's structure and aesthetics. For example, learning about ocean acoustics and the description of the SOFAR channel from Visiting Professor of Physical Oceanography and Climate Carl Wunsch helped PearlDamour decide music's key role in the production.[9] They also chose to anthropomorphize the ocean and worked with three different performers known for their gender-queer devising work – Taylor Mac, Daniel Alexander Jones, and Jennifer Kidwell – to articulate the shape, dynamics, and tone of this being. Finally, inspired by the 2013 actions of Texas state senator Wendy Davis, the loose narrative structure became a filibuster, a tool of political debate often heralded as either the final bulwark against controversial legislation via tactics of delay and debate or a procedural manipulation that exacerbates gridlock and supports minority over majority rule.[10]

Dominion and Dominance,Symbiosis and Synthesis

In a nod to tangled systems of governance, PearlDamour sets *Ocean*'s action in the "future global senate chamber of 2050" where "Mr. Majority" brings to the floor "The End of Ocean" bill that proposes,

> Wherefore The Ocean, she has descended into unfathomable chaos and wherefore New York City is now a small island of memorials accessed by ferry and Osaka is a deep-water tourist attraction accessed by submersible musk mobiles and wherefore the seat of global government is now split between Geneva and Seattle, we, the members of the Global Senate beg all those who love life to come together as a people to solve the most pressing problem of our time.

Mr. Majority then paints a picture of our "grand old watery Grandma" Ocean, diseased, disoriented, "horribly sick," "barely breathing." Her death, as prescribed by the bill, would be a kindness. It would also allow humans to reclaim land for development. This imagined legislation is a politician's attempt to dominate the earth through human will while also deflecting the role human actions have played in the earth's destruction. Mr. Majority pitches a plan created by the Senate, working with "world-class scientists, biologists, and engineers" to "drain the Ocean's depleted waters into caverns deep inside the Earth's crust" while the "sick water" is diverted via "zero-gravity chutes, transported beyond our atmosphere, and released into OUTER SPACE!"[11] He displays a video of a twenty-fifth-century Pangea with seven new "pristine, manageable seas" that represent "better versions of the Ocean that we can nurture with intention and, yes, love." There is hyperbole at work here but also the chilling reality of disaster capitalism that sees opportunity for the few in the catastrophe for many. Mr. Majority touts the new terra-formed seabed organized around our "favorite landmarks," where tourist attractions will flourish (such as "rock climbing on the Great Barrier Reef" or "bicycl[ing] the scenic Florida-Cuba trail"), and he sings a hymn to a new era of Manifest Destiny:

> You'll watch your sons and daughters as they populate this land.
> No more troubled Oceans, only placid lakes and streams.
> Refineries and wheat fields as far as you can see.
> No more sinking, no more swimming.

You can ask for more.
No more drowning in self-pity. It's time for you to soar.

Just as he feels he's conjured up the suitable sentiment for a positive vote, Mr. Majority confronts an unanticipated constituent: the Ocean.

"What would it mean for the ocean to talk until it is heard?" became an animating question for the team. In the current touring production, Jennifer Kidwell plays both the Ocean and Mr. Majority in a battle for the floor of the chamber and for the attention of the audience. As D'Amour explained in a 2020 Guggenheim Works & Process showing, having legislator and ocean in one actor makes physically manifest an interconnectivity that goes unremarked in our daily lives. Although humans are dependent on the ocean in physiological as well as geographical ways, most of us have a limited concept of how much influence the ocean has on the ways of life on land. In reviews of the A.R.T. premiere, some critics seem frustrated and confused by this duality in performance (Sinclair), while others read this choice as "underlin[ing] the interconnected nature of the relationship between humans and the ocean" (Wallenberg). Instead of a scientist representing the facts and figures about ocean acidity, sea level rise, or microplastics, the Ocean speaks for itself and its constituents, a myriad of creatures and features.[12] While Mr. Majority wants to drain and split the Ocean for means of control, at the end of part 1 the Ocean realizes that the solitary human body/voice and perspective in which they have chosen to communicate is too confining, too unlike their fluid state. Consequently, they split into what D'Amour calls their "other ocean selves, essentially a choir." The company casts this ensemble from the locations where the production tours. These local actors provide the shared Ocean voice for part 2, and in the play's final moments, they join Kidwell in a hocketing round, sharing the story of a whale's call to a mate across the SOFAR channel lost against the incessant traffic of commercial, military, and private watercraft.[13]

After intermission, the Ocean pauses the filibuster and the human experience of time and concept of space. Whereas part 1 bounces back and forth between Mr. Majority and the Ocean, part 2 is set "in my Ocean mind," and the perspective is not one presented in/with/for human comfort. An expansive video projection conveys details from the HUCE scientists' research as the Ocean presents a series of counterarguments to Mr. Majority that discuss status, risk, and remedy. These concerns mirror those of communities most affected by environmental racism. PearlDamour often takes the Global South as a grounding location where global majority communities remain dependent on the extractive economic entities that also destroy the spaces/places where they live either through active pollution or passive policy neglect.[14] Mr. Majority's legislation foregrounds privileged countries and people, seeking justice from the more-than-human world. But the Ocean notes our situation emerges from eons of extraction, domination, and possession. We are out of sync with the water, the air, and the land, and the Ocean sings about how these will go on without us:

> I don't care about you.
> You act the Goliath.
> Stomp your feet and beat your chest. It's just another day.
> Don't pretend to care.
> Don't fill me with your dread.
> Don't dip your toes in me and sigh, "Don't look at me that way."
> I don't care about you.

The Ocean invites us to see from the perspective of sea creatures, to feel a different rhythm and flow of life, one we fight against at our own peril. But the dynamic represents an interesting challenge for audiences: see yourself reflected in this fantastical personification who appears utterly detached from your outcome. The Ocean will exist in one way or another, but whether it remains a resource to support our living, the answer to that question is up to us.

Audience participation is built into *Ocean* performances. Prior to attending, during, or even without attending at all, you can download an augmented reality app, *Deep Wonder*, which allows you to scan the floor wherever you are and experience features of the ocean floor constructed from HUCE scientific data. A digitized program and interactive intermission extend the time spent with scientific research and water/ocean advocacy efforts drawn together by the show's topic.[15] PearlDamour collaborates with local environmental advocacy groups at their tour locations for specific environmental content to convey and actions for audiences to take. It remains to be seen how *Ocean*'s multivocality might nudge audiences across very different experiences (geographic, educational, generational) toward solidarity and a more holistic relationship with water, air, and land. Such a transformation will require a significant reconfiguration of embedded ideas, even within science, away from these materials as resources toward these materials as collaborators. To that end, *Ocean* pushes the boundaries of character coherence and point of view to help audiences flex creative interpretive muscles needed for the work ahead.

Scientist as Citizen Artist

Laura J. Moore, professor of coastal geomorphology at the University of North Carolina at Chapel Hill, contacted me in 2016 with a desire to change the way she communicated her research about the barrier islands that make up the majority of North Carolina's coastline. These islands are both valuable real estate along the East and Gulf Coasts and increasingly vulnerable to sea level rise. In the short term, developers and tourist-dependent coastal communities replenish the sand or (re)build roads and seawalls when they are washed away by storms. This approach artificially holds the shoreline and the island in place, which seems like a positive strategy given that

> as sea level rises or sediment supply rates decrease, a barrier island will respond by (1) migrating landward across the underlying substrate to higher elevations, (2) disintegrating if there is no longer sufficient sand volume and relief above sea level to prevent inundation during storms, or (3) drowning in place and transforming into a marine sand body.
> (Moore et al. 1)

Moore and her colleagues have found that replenishing the shorelines actually has negative impacts on the landforms' complex, natural processes, which are unique based on barrier islands' varied coastal geographies. Moore's research uses "morphological-behavior modeling" systems to chart the evolution of barrier islands "throughout the Holocene" (Moore et al. 2) and assesses various factors such as "sea level rise rate, sediment supply rate, shoreface depth, substrate composition, substrate erodibility and maximum shoreface erosion rate" for "a range of time scales and in realistically complex scenarios where multiple parameters are changing at the same time" (15). Moore wants North Carolinians to recognize this complexity so we might trace its effects beyond a single generation in the past as well as look further ahead than just the next 15–20 years. Industries and municipalities, however, tend to make decisions focused on immediate profits, preservations, and an image of beach life that centers leisure activities. Ironically, such an ideal is only possible due to geological formations that evolved without large-scale human impact or interventions. Some of the more drastic measures to preserve the islands' current states artificially and prioritize private property might ultimately eliminate beaches as we know them (Cooper and Pilkey).

Moore has advocated for collaborative research and public engagement throughout her academic career. She initially considered a documentary theater approach and began work with Kathryn Hunter Williams, faculty in the Department of Dramatic Art and the cofounder of Hidden Voices, a community-based theater company that often builds plays from interviews and story circles. Moore and Williams received a Fostering Interdisciplinary Research Explorations (FIRE) grant from the university to travel to the Texas coast and meet with individuals who had experienced Hurricanes Ike and Rita and chose either to stay/rebuild or move. For Moore, that trip to the Bolivar Peninsula illuminated a few key tensions. First, individual and community investment (money and generational ties) in living and/or working on barrier islands will not be ceded easily. Scientific involvement usually arrives alongside government intervention, thus linking them together as pitted against the interests of local/regional industries and communities dependent on those industries. Second, the budgets of federal buyout programs targeting restoration pale in comparison to money offered from developers, and both propel the choices of those without personal wealth to rebuild as they resist abandoning threatened homes/businesses during severe storms even at the cost of their lives. Finally, a community's ability to prioritize the future over the present and to reckon with the past poses one of the highest hurdles to collaborative measures toward long-term nourishment of these landforms. Nostalgia for a type of beach lifestyle has always been tinged with racial and economic restrictions, though it is marketed as available to/desirable for all. The mathematical models on which geologists depend can produce abstract and complex information that quickly surpasses a layperson's comprehension. Such technical language is no match for the perceived simplicity of love for sand and surf. This constructed tranquility of beach living as always fair weathered also denies the reality of coastal life with its "full range of vulnerability as natural and inevitable."[16] News stories that show entire communities washed away after a storm are quickly exchanged for the hum of rebuilding efforts and "once-in-a-lifetime storm" rhetorical flourishes that try to put disaster in the rearview mirror.

***Rollover*: Connecting Present to Future**

Ultimately, Moore decided against a documentary theater approach, preferring to combine aspects of the Texas interviews with her own fieldwork in New Jersey and North Carolina and write a kitchen sink drama about a fictional family, the Irvings, living and working for multiple generations in Rollover, a fictional Gulf Coast town. The family has gained and shed members over various drafts; currently, the play's central action focuses on half-siblings – William (Bill) and Leena – who evacuate their elderly mother from their family home because of one of these "once-in-a-lifetime" storms, one in which Bill almost perishes. The matriarch's return (or not) to the home must be decided by the children. Since the grant-writing process for development support is ongoing and represents interdisciplinary complexities, some dramaturgical decisions reflect both Moore's research and NSF reviewer's concerns about how to accurately assess the play's impact on public attitudes. Bill and Leena represent different community points of view and decision-making power. Leena, a coastal geologist not unlike the playwright, teaches at a university inland having used her hometown as a field site for many years, urging locals to take a more proactive stance on coastal living under climate change. Bill, a deputy chief firefighter and emergency preparedness official of the town, has been caring for their mother since her cancer diagnosis. The family home will pass to him upon his mother's death, and he speaks about legacy in a town where they are one of only a handful of multiracial families to have weathered social and economic struggles. The storm that severely damages their home and levels much of the town reverses their roles. Leena becomes single-mindedly focused on rebuilding the home so that their mother can return. After nearly drowning in an attempt to save a longtime resident who refused to evacuate, Bill pushes to detangle the family from the cycle of destruction and development that has increasingly prioritized tourists over natural spaces and year-round residents.

Moore has given *Rollover* a fairly standard plot: as two children with divergent life experiences struggle over how to care for an ill and aging parent, their decisions are intensified by an environmental disaster that throws the entire community into crisis. The development team's hope has been that shared questions of mortality, legacy, and economics could invite discussion about the shifts required for coastal communities to imagine a different relationship with land, place, and time.[17] Noting that the fate of developed coastal landforms depends on management decisions made decades prior, Moore also includes a framing story set in 2050 where Future Leena has guided the Rollover community through an eventual transition of the land back to a more undeveloped state. Future Leena appears throughout the play's action, moving the audience back and forth through time, navigating a collection of objects that become touchstones for the family's decision-making. She also deconstructs the Irving family home, which remains a skeleton of a once-modest dwelling in order to forestall nostalgic assumptions about the ease of rebuilding. Future Leena also incorporates a preshow detail that allows the play to connect with specific audiences across anticipated production locations. Attendees are asked to describe an object that holds pride of place in their home however they define that idea. Responses are selected at random right before curtain and incorporated by the Future Leena actor as the remnants of Rollover's community members contribute to a shared structure that holds their memories in a now much-reduced footprint of "home."

Assessing Interdependence as Impact

In the six years (2015–2022) *Rollover* has been in development, the creative team has charted the changing public and federal policy dynamic regarding science and arts funding. NSF funding has been the primary goal so that Moore might receive support for her playwrighting as a form of scientific knowledge production.[18] As "climate change musical" and "NSF waste" talking points reappeared in conservative and mainstream news coverage after the 2016 election, the team decided to implement a contrasting experience to measure audience impact. Moore added collaborators in engineering and computer science to craft a companion virtual reality (VR) experience, *Shelter in Place*, to simulate storm surge entering and rising within a coastal home, echoing Bill's near-death experience. This supplement would allow the development team to measure two differently embodied experiences: the first-person immersion of VR and the third-person communal immersion of theater.[19] The team expanded to include social scientists with expertise in STEM communication and informal education outcomes to spearhead the creation of pre-performance, post-performance, and long-range surveys and quantitative measures of attitudinal shifts. We worked to balance claims that multiple, integrated embodied experiences can positively inform about climate change that will transform the U.S. coasts while also ensuring evaluators we would not use science to advocate for specific outcomes:

> Critically, *Rollover* and *Shelter in Place* do not advocate for a particular future. Rather, they are designed to be "honest brokers" (Pielke, 2007), communicating the complexity of coupled natural-human dynamics to promote learning and informed engagement in personal and community-level decision making that is intentional in its vision, whatever that vision may be.[20]

Even as research shows specific positive outcomes for a human inhabitant–limited approach to coastal management, our grant language focused on the ways the project would "leverage emotion to enable content understanding and close the knowledge-intention-action gap," leaving the "action" part of desired outcomes generic. We hoped to provide a model for development that other interdisciplinary groups could replicate while taking up different dimensions of the multipronged approach necessary for climate change engagements.[21] As of this writing, our efforts to secure this large-scale funding for the project has been unsuccessful.

In the evidence collected and cited to demonstrate *Rollover*'s roots in scientific research, the foundation for our hypothesis of its potential effectiveness on public attitudes, and the quantitative measures planned to analyze its reception, our submission materials could not include the full script. Such a restriction marks a logical limit given the scientific context for proposals and reviewers, yet it also illustrates how disciplinary authority affects the approach to assess interdisciplinary collaboration and production. In our rejections so far, it has been difficult to deduce exactly which elements are lacking and whether residual concerns remain about funding theatrical work even as other interactive or immersive performance-oriented proposals gain support.[22] Similarly, in the conservative press coverage of *The Great Immensity*'s NSF funding, there is no mention of the multimethod study they required of the play's impact based on its run at the Kansas City Repertory Theater. Independent consultant Ellen Giusti provided this report in August 2012 using the agency's own *Framework for Evaluating Impacts of Informal Science Education Projects.* Whereas pundits and politicians characterized the funding as "waste," institutional assessment metrics were followed and judged to be in line with informal education event expectations.

For this mixed-methods study, Guisti observed multiple performances (including student matinees) and a post-show discussion and analyzed the theater's online survey (with a 43% return rate) for adult patrons with 13 questions about their experience and 5 demographic questions. She concluded that audiences agreed that the format of a play can "reach people who think they can't understand science," and the use of music made "the science exciting and understandable for non-scientists" (3). According to the NSF's categories of impact, italicized here as they appeared in Guisti's summary, the play "*engaged* two widely diverse audiences [adults and students] and *increased understanding* of the topics involved" (33). While *attitudes* toward what can be done about the "ecological crisis" remained largely unchanged, student respondents wanted "to learn more about what they personally can do" (19), and both students and adult patrons agreed that "individuals can have a positive impact on the environment," with adults arguing they were doing "all they could" even as they categorized their *behavior* as "green when it's easy" (31). Specific *skills* acquired from engaging the show and its programming were more elusive as Guisti found audiences were largely unaware of "the progressive approach [to environmental problems] their city is taking" (33). The chance to learn these details from local experts who appeared in post-show discussions meant that "the arts have the potential to reach audiences that science lectures and journals cannot" (33). Guisti also cites the play's website as a key means to extend any awareness inspired in audience members and ways to reach individuals who might not see the play in full but could learn from the elements of its plot inspired by scientific research (32). Nowhere in her report does Guisti imply that the production wasted funds or fell short of its goals regarding informal science education impact.

As Steve Cosson noted in a 2020 interview with Elizabeth Bennett for the *Stage Directors and Choreographers Journal*, the criticism leveled at The Civilians' receipt of NSF funding was not unexpected. Cosson had weathered political attacks on the arts before, having written grants during the days of the "NEA Four" controversy and virulent "anti-gay, anti-sex, and anti-feminist" attitudes in government in the 1990s (41). He was still dismayed, however, when *The Great Immensity*'s website was "hacked and taken out" (42) and a new wave of conservative and mainstream media revived "climate change musical" stories as the then-Representative Lamar Smith (R-TX) became the chair of the House's Science Committee in 2013. Smith campaigned on his effort to stamp out "waste" at the NSF and his own climate change denial made *The Great Immensity* a perfect symbol of his criticism that the Obama administration had "politicized" science. Smith's efforts were minimized by other congressional actors, but the 2016 election ushered in an entire administration eager to cut government spending on the arts *and* the sciences and another round of now "*failed* climate change musical" stories returned to the mediascape. Beyond feeling personally abandoned by both the NSF and national arts agencies, Cosson reminded Bennett that the ongoing and largely uncontradicted critique of public funding for interdisciplinary work undermines new work development from artists who already scale difficult silos built around knowledge, communication, and validity (42–43). Even so, Harvard's commission of PearlDamour, Princeton's initial grant to The Civilians, Fondakowski's invitation to co-teach at

Wesleyan, and Moore's continued pursuit of *Rollover*'s development funds from science research and education sources demonstrate that citizen scientists and citizen artists find their way to each other across the "two cultures" divide with a commitment to doing and learning alongside each other and the wider public. Such common efforts allow theater projects the means to counter a force operating more stealthily in C.P. Snow's equation: the third culture of governance that affects both science and art.

Notes

1 A 2018 *Nature* article, "No PhD Needed," places the practice's global origins in ancient China where farmers tracked the migration of crop-destroying locusts for thousands of years.

2 Haklay's ordering of citizen science project participation echoes Kazzazi's division of the different roles science plays in science plays discussed in chapter 1.

3 All quotes from *SPILL* are from the publicly available LA Theatre Works *Relativity* series recording, marked with part 1 or 2 and a time stamp from the Soundcloud recording.

4 Chernoff pursued this collaboration one year after establishing the university's College of the Environment and four years after Wesleyan's Center for the Arts joined the first iteration of the Doris Duke Charitable Trust's Creative Campus Innovations grant.

5 Fishery employment data taken from "Eat Safe Louisiana."

6 *Milton* resulted in a published text, which contains portions of a central script, but instead of providing a blueprint to re-create this specific work, it offers a set of stories and provocations about such arts projects as a whole. This summary of questions is from a section titled "Dramaturgy of Participation."

7 *Milton* continues to host spectators via a website, https://www.skyovermilton.com/, that houses audio/video/story chronicles of the various community performances.

8 Quotes from the artists involved in *Ocean Filibuster* are from viewings or workshop performances via Vimeo and Zoom. Quotes from the performance are from its opening on March 2, 2022 at American Repertory Theatre viewed remotely.

9 See the NOAA's "What Is SOFAR?" explainer for details about ocean acoustics.

10 Davis made international headlines when she spoke for 13 hours standing without food or drink to forestall an anti-abortion bill in the Texas legislature.

11 While seemingly the stuff of science fiction, during the Works & Progress Zoom presentation, D'Amour revealed the outer space solution was the brainchild of scientist Carl Wunsch who expanded an "artistic" invention with elements of scientific feasibility.

12 When asked about pronouns, the Ocean responds with "O." Even though Mr. Majority genders the Ocean female, as is sea-faring tradition, given

the Ocean's discussion of fluidity and the "fiction" of boundaries as well as Kidwell's personal use of she/they, I use they/them when referencing the Ocean character within this chapter.

13 Hocketing is a vocal and compositional device wherein melodies and rhythm are redistributed among voices or instruments, requiring intensive concentration and collaboration among any ensemble performing its precise mechanics.

14 D'Amour is from New Orleans, and Pearl is from Tulsa.

15 At A.R.T., they collaborated with the Conservation Law Foundation, Bow Seat Ocean Awareness Programs, and Mass Audubon.

16 This phrasing is from an October 2015 Google Doc free-write by Moore.

17 At two public showings in April 2018 and March 2022, central North Carolina audiences had lively discussions about the difficulty of decision-making and the increasing pressure they felt regarding climate change even though many did not live full time on the coast.

18 During this time, Moore has maintained a full-time teaching load and pursued a rigorous disciplinary research agenda, including directing the NSF-funded Collaboratory for Coastal Adaptation over Space and Time (https://c-coast.org/).

19 We were bolstered in this addition when we heard of PearlDamour's planned AR app for *Ocean Filibuster*.

20 This is language from our 2019 grant proposal.

21 Moore continues to pursue revisions, staged readings, and proposals geared toward other STEM funding entities.

22 Advanced Informal STEM Learning/NSF funded a 2017 grant for just under $1 million to support faculty at the Pratt Institute and Oregon State University seeking to study/improve practices around incorporating STEM learning into cultural events using a model that "integrates science with art, music, and play, producing live events, games, hands-on workshops, and interactive theater productions" (https://www.nsf.gov/awardsearch/showAward?AWD_ID=1612719). See Rosin et al. for a discussion of the results.

References

Bennett, Elizabeth. "Interview with Steve Cosson." *Stage Directors and Choreographers Journal*, vol. 8, no. 2, 19 May 2020, pp. 41–43.

Brown, Paul. "Ecological Knowledge in Community Theater." *CLCWeb: Comparative Literature and Culture*, vol. 16, no. 4, 2001. doi:10.7771/1481-4374.2584.

Chaudhuri, Una. "'There Must Be a Lot of Fish in That Lake': Toward an Ecological Theater." *Theater*, vol. 25, no. 1, 1994, pp. 23–31.

"Climate Beneath the Surface." *Shakespeare and Company Theater & Policy Salon*. Zoom event, 21 Apr. 2021.

Cooper, Caren B., and Bruce V. Lewenstein. "Two Meanings of Citizen Science." *The Rightful Place of Science: Citizen Science*, edited by D. Cavalier. University of Arizona Press, 2016, pp. 51–62.

Cooper, J., Andrew, G., and Orrin H. Pilkey, editors. *Pitfalls of Shoreline Stabilization: Selected Case Studies*. Springer, 2012. doi:10.1007/978-94-007-4123-2.

Curiel, Himeka. "Citizen Artist: Creating Social Engaged Theater as Civic Practice." *Wesleyan University Magazine*, 24 Sept. 2020. magazine.blogs.wesleyan.edu/2020/09/24/citizen-artist-creating-socially-engaged-theater-as-civic-practice/.

D'Amour, Lisa, Katie Pearl, and Kate Kremer. *Milton: A Performance and Community Engagement Experiment*. 53rd State Press, 2019.

"Eat Safe, Louisiana: Commercial Seafood." Louisiana Department of Health, 2010. ldh.la.gov/page/444#~:text=With%20annual%20retail%2C%20i.mport%20and,jobs·*%20for%20commercial%20seafood%20alone.

"Factsheet on BP Vessels of Opportunity Program." *PR Web/CISON*. 1997–2015, 7 Jul. 2010. www1.prweb.com/prfiles/2010/11/16/4215244/factsheetbpvooprogram070710.pdf.

Fondakowski, Leah. *SPILL*. L.A. Theatre Works. Relativity Series. latw.org/title/spill.

Gioia, Michael. "Leigh Fondakowski's SPILL, about the BP oil spill, will have world premiere in Louisiana." *Playbill.org*, 10 Dec. 2013. playbill.com/article/leigh-fondakowskis-spill-about-the-bp-oil-spill-will-have-world-premiere-in-louisiana-com-212664.

Guggenheim Museum. *Ocean Filibuster: Virtual Works & Process*. Zoom, 8 June 2020.

Guisti, Ellen. "*The Great Immensity*: Conveying Science Through the Performing Arts, an Assessment." *InformalScience.org*, Aug. 2012. www.informalscience.org/sites/default/files/The_Great_Immensity_Summative.Eval.Final.pdf.

Haklay, Muki. "Citizen Science and Volunteered Geographic Information: Overview and Typology of Participation." *Crowdsourcing Geographic Knowledge*, edited by Daniel Sui et al., Springer, 2013, pp. 105–122. https://doi.org/10.1007/978-94-007-4587-2_7.

Haklay, Muki. "Participatory Citizen Science." *Citizen Science: Innovation in Open Science, Society and Policy*, edited by Muki Haklay et al., UCL Press, 2018, pp. 52–62. jstor.org/stable/j.ctv550cf2.11.

Highsaw, Carol A. *A Theatre of Action: The Living Newspapers of the Federal Theatre Project*. 1988. Princeton University, PhD dissertation. proquest.com/dissertations-theses/theatre-action-living-newspapers-federal-project/docview/303745307/se-2.

Hirsh, Deborah. "*The Great Immensity* at KC Rep Takes on Global Warming." *The Pitch*, 29 Feb. 2012. www.thepitchkc.com/the-great-immensity-at-kc-rep-takes-on-global-warming/.

Irwin, Aisling. "No PhDs Needed: How Citizen Science Is Transforming Research." *Nature*, 23 Oct. 2018. www.nature.com/articles/d41586-018-07106-5/.

Irwin, Alan. *Citizen Science: A Study of People, Expertise, and Sustainable Development*. Routledge, 1995.

Kaufman, Moises, et al. *Moment Work: Tectonic Theater Project's Process of Devising Theater*. Vintage, 2018.

Moore, Laura J. *Rollover.* Unpublished manuscript. University of North Carolina Process Series Version Mar. 2022.

Moore, Laura J., et al. "Complexities in Barrier Island Response to Sea Level Rise: Insights from Numerical Model Experiments, North Carolina Outer Banks." *Journal of Geophysical Research*, vol. 115, 2010, F03004. doi:10.1029/2009JF001299.

Myer, Robinson. "Geology's Timekeepers Are Feuding." *The Atlantic.com*, July 2018. theatlantic.com/science/archive/2018/07/anthropocene-holocene-geology-drama/565628/.

NOAA. "What Is SOFAR?" National Ocean Service. oceanservice.noaa.gov/facts/sofar.html.

Odendahl-James, Jules. "The Science of Dramaturgy and the Dramaturgy of Science." *Routledge Companion to Dramaturgy*, edited by Magda Romanska, Routledge, 2015, pp. 381–387.

Pearl/Damour. *Ocean Filibuster.* American Repertory Theater. Cambridge, MA. Livestream recorded 2 Mar. 2022. Viewed 25 Mar. 2022.

Pearl, Katie. "*Ocean Filibuster* Work Sample." Abrons Arts Center Workshop, Dec. 2018. Vimeo.

Pearl, Katie. "We Are Climate." *HowlRound.com.* 16 Apr. 2017. howlround.com/we-are-climate.

Powers, PJ. "A Conversation with Leigh Fondakowski." *Timelinetheatre.com*, 2 Dec. 2015. timelinetheatre.com/2015/12/conversation-leigh-fondakowski/.

Reinelt, Janelle. "The Promise of Documentary." *Get Real: Documentary Theatre Past and Present*, edited by Alison Forsyth and Chris Megson. Palgrave Macmillan, 2009, pp. 6–23.

Rohd, Michael. "The New Work of Building Civic Practice." *HowlRound.com*, 9 July 2012. howlround.com/new-work-building-civic-practice.

Rosin, Mark S., et al. "Broadening Participation in Science Through Arts-Facilitated Experiences at a Cultural Festival." *PLoS One*, vol. 18, 2023. doi:10.1371/journal. pone.0284432.

Sinclair, Jacquinn. "*Ocean Filibuster* Mimics Real-Life Climate Change Politics on Stage." *WBUR Boston*, 4 Mar. 2022. www.wbur.org/news/2022/3/04/american-repertory-theater-ocean-filibuster-review.

Troeh, Eve. "Deepwater, Center-Stage: Disaster Through Survivors Eyes." *All Things Considered*, 18 Mar. 2014. www.npr.org/2014/03/18/291172169/deepwater-center-stage-disaster-as-told-by-those-who-were-there.

Trumbull, Deborah J., et al. "Thinking Scientifically During Participation in a Citizen-Science Project." *Science Education*, vol. 84, no. 2, 2000, pp. 265–275.

Wallenberg, Christopher. "In A.R.T.'s Ocean Filibuster, an Argument for a Sea Change with a Bit of Spectacle." *Boston Globe*, 24 Feb. 2022. bostonglobe.com/2022/02/24/arts/arts-ocean-filibuster-an-argument-sea-change-with-bit-spectacle/.

Wesleyan University Center for the Arts. "Talk by Leigh Fondakowski on Her Work, SPILL." *YouTube*, 30 Oct. 2014. youtu.be/3QcMG0LhCeU.

4 Dramaturgy of Precarity

Instrument and Insight

Among theater practitioners, both technology and dramaturgy can be considered as tools implemented or applied toward larger products and processes. Technologists and dramaturgs often resist these characterizations, arguing that each practice is a conceptual, creative domain in its own right. In some sense, this duality between and within dramaturgy and technology reflects a central tension in the "two cultures" divide. Is the art in SciArt the employment of representational skills for the communication of the *real* knowledge, science? Is the science that informs SciArt's world building so abstracted or so transformed/translated through artistic collaborations as to be disciplinarily meaningless?[1] Artist Andrew Yang answers these questions in this way: "If art-science projects were to cleanly meet the standard of either discipline, they would simply duplicate that disciplines' work, not experiment with its forms or test the edges or standards of practice" (318). Such questions and answers sit at the core of how art and science are conceptualized as products instead of quintessential human actions: to wonder, to create, and to collaborate.

Theater history itself can be told as a narrative of interweaving technological and dramaturgical changes. In the *Cambridge Guide to Science and Theater* (2020) for which she also serves as editor, Shepherd-Barr offers a historiography of nineteenth-century theater technologies where patents emerged from theater laborers' applied science experimentations with materials. She considers the ways in which theater production offered a proving ground for the hypothesis-driven work of inventors, engineers, and artists, as well as a "complex interrelationship of aesthetic innovation and technological change" (214). If theater historians and practitioners note this complexity, she argues, we must consider the "role we assign to the scientific and mechanical

DOI: 10.4324/9781003150848-5

factors[2] that enabled and perhaps caused artistic or literary change" (213–214). In this twenty-first-century moment, with theater enmeshed with digital technologies that provide new opportunities for performance, it could be easy to forget that technology-informed dramaturgical experimentation has existed for hundreds of years. Such experimentation influences the ways playwrights imagine worlds that are realized through the staging process, informs the ways in which audiences and critics receive those worlds, and sets the stage for new work. Technology provides mechanisms, domains, and dynamics that expand human experience through what Harvard's metaLAB Future Stage Research Group calls "liveness plus," a new domain and process of development that "open[s] up new horizons of experience for audience and performers; experiences from hitherto unimaginable angles and on hitherto unimaginable perceptual time scales; events designed to add value to each and every channel that structures the experience" (future-stage.org/). Technology-informed dramaturgy and dramaturgically informed "liveness plus" storytelling also influences the scholarship that evaluates creators' innovations. This trajectory repeats in other adjacent art forms. In his introduction to *Digital Performance: A History of New Media in Theater, Dance, Performance Art and Installation*, Steve Dixon quotes critical media scholar R.L. Rutsky's observation of the mid-twentieth-century shift in avant-garde film and architecture from the "notion of technology as instrumental, as the functional application of science" to "a conception that sees technology as a matter of form, of representation" (8).

Such interplay drives artists' dramaturgical production practices and critical analyses. One particular domain of interrogation has to do with what constitutes a text. If one accepts that a fundamental focus of dramaturgical analysis is the text from which performance springs, as the boundaries of "text" change, so do dramaturgy's terrains, techniques, and analytic languages. Although not all of theater's technology-influenced products are postdramatic, the postdramatic has been an arena of theater frequently associated with the influence of or built using the languages of technology. "In postdramatic theatre, performance art and dance, the traditional hierarchy of theatrical elements has almost vanished," note Hans-Thies Lehmann and Patrick Primavesi (3). They argue that in a contemporary moment influenced by "a global media culture," theater need not "copy media technologies" writ large or maintain "a defensive ontology of live 'presence.'" Instead, dramaturgical practice can "negotiate for the freedom of theatrical experimentation and risk," thinking and acting with technological contexts, influences, materials "as an experimentalist" working within a production to uncover the language of rehearsal and presentation (4).

Of relevance to science theater collaborations is Lehmann and Primavesi's caution against dramaturgy's enlightenment impulses. They advocate for dramaturgs to work toward "a political way of making art," "transgress[ing] traditional definitions," and forging "a strategy of communication" versus presenting a product for consumption (5, 6). This vision for the field and its practices is echoed by Michael Chemers and Michael Sell in their idea of "systemic dramaturgy," which considers theater's

> interlocking set of conceptual systems: interpretive systems, production systems, teaching systems, and research systems. The systemic dramaturg understands not only how these systems work but also how they work together and how they work in concert with larger ongoing systems including aesthetic, political, and economic ones.
>
> (25)

Chemers and Sell are interested in how more expansive historiographies might illuminate challenges and opportunities for theater/performance that do not reinscribe narratives of suspicion regarding technology as demonstrative of Western cultures' modern or postmodern alienation from materiality. Instead, their vision for "systemic dramaturgy" includes global and preindustrial moments and locations, allowing the field to find dramaturgy "within a much broader conceptual framework that considers not just technology but *tekne*," the art of bringing form into being and, by extension, into systems of meaning (41).

This idea of "systemic dramaturgy" seems akin to a vision of "two cultures" collaboration that Bruno Latour imagines as a flow of considerations that runs between art and science: "A matter of concern is what happens to a matter of fact when you add to it its whole scenography, much like you would do by shifting your attention from the stage to the whole machinery of a theatre" (39). In recent science communication studies, researchers argue that the size and scope of troubling events, particularly surrounding environmental issues and public health, can overwhelm individuals who are increasingly driven by political affiliations and perspectives demanded by said affiliations. Emotion – from humor to pathos – can interrupt the confirmatory loop of information and provide a window for education.[3] There are now myriad programs and projects to train scientists in communication strategies – improvisation, personal narrative, documentary-oriented photography and filmmaking, interviews and podcasts – packaging storytelling structures for deployment.[4] Shared research from which representation might spring remains rarer. As *The Great Immensity*'s cultural impact demonstrates, STEAM collaborations are scrutinized by networks far outside disciplinary fields and, in recent years, must also contend with growing dis- and misinformation media campaigns, themselves facilitated by the speed, reach, and employment of technological tools and social media networks that can target artists and scientists and subject them to unanticipated critiques with diminished public platforms to refute successfully.

This does not mean that experimental, collaborative projects do not find ways to exist. In fact, the SciArt domains of digital art, electronic composition, dance-theater, and site-specific performance have engaged in lively conversation for decades with technological research and tools of making. Chemers and Sell offer dramaturgs training for these worlds in their *Systemic Dramaturgy: A Handbook for the Digital Age* (2022), and this chapter explores some of the porous boundaries between theater/performance and other visual and performing arts forms discussing how collaborations, particularly those that employ digital technology as a language and platform of creation, engage a **dramaturgy of precarity** that undergirds their making, reception, and assessment processes.

First, this chapter surveys the landscape carved by the journal *Leonardo*, one of the few peer-reviewed spaces for artists working in collaboration with science and technology and vice versa. In *Leonardo*, inter- and transdisciplinary projects abound, many with the support of institutionally anchored research and development spaces or a robust cultural sector and international government funding to support risky ideas. I examine how the category of "SciArt" within *Leonardo*'s pages has expanded and contracted over the past decade[5] and look briefly at the relatively recent practice of embedding or inviting artists into science labs (in a version of how S.T.A.G.E. is organized). While he has not made many appearances in *Leonardo*'s pages, the chapter turns to "rhythm scientist" Paul D. Miller (a.k.a. DJ Spooky the Subliminal Kid), who, like playwright Lauren Gunderson, has forged a range of commercial and experimental SciArt partnerships. Miller's climate change-oriented pieces also navigate an increasingly precarious planetary future. Finally, since this book bears the signs of being written during a global pandemic, it seemed fitting to engage theater making with technology that emerged when theater houses were closed. To that end, this chapter concludes with a look at the performances of Theater in Quarantine and their analog-digital flow of practice that centers the physical body through remote and digital technologies. TiQ harkens back to mid-1960s experimental art and performance while challenging the conditions of twenty-first-century theatrical production and reception, pulling the curtain back on technological tools and offering audiences a chance to engage precarity in productive ways and forge a digitally facilitated animacy for these times.

Of Polymaths and Paths of Influence

Leonardo da Vinci looms large as the SciArt polymath par excellence whose influence on the realms of imagination, creation, and experimentation draw science and art together in harmonious union.[6] *Leonardo* journal founder, rocket scientist and kinetic sculptor Frank Malina, may have anticipated the value already placed on the artist Leonardo's range of interests and influences and hoped the name would resonate with both artists and scientists. Calling it *Malina* might not have had the same unifying effect, though the trajectory of Malina's life and career speaks volumes about the systems that permeate the "two cultures." His eldest son, Roger, has served as executive editor of the journal since 1982, and in a 2017 interview with *Medium*, Roger described the lengths to which his father, the son of immigrants from what is now Czechia, pursued his interests in rocket design during the 1940s and '50s, funding his studies as the operator of CalTech's wind tunnel for aeronautics research and as an illustrator of his Ph.D. mentor's textbooks (LaMont). He founded his first company, Aerojet Corporation, when his research team was ejected from the university due to explosions caused by their rocket engine tests (Pendle).

According to his son, the elder Malina strove to expand scientific research in universities with government funding but found Cold War politics restrictive of intellectual freedom. Exiled from the United States during the late 1950s, he shifted his full-time attention to art. With ample funds from the sale of Aerojet, he founded a group of Kinetic Art creators in Paris, integrating technology into visual art in ways that pushed beyond cinematic and photographic dominance of the early twentieth century. Roger Malina notes that his father wanted to be a part of a new moment in art production "that took advantage of the technology available to the artists for their purposes but also took the landscape that science explored, the ideas that science brought to the table" (LaMont). When he returned to the States in the

1960s, Frank Malina found other individuals who merged their backgrounds in the arts and the sciences such as engineer Billy Kluver and sculptor Jean Tiguely who would form E.A.T., or Experiments in Art and Technology (Glueck). He initially thought to make an organization or club but settled on

> a magazine where artists could write about their own work in the same way scientists write about their work … a place where artists could document their technical ideas but also talk about their research methodology and what they were trying to do in the same way scientists did.
>
> (LaMont)

Leonardo has published a global array of scholarship for over 50 years now, including a recent (2019) higher education institutional partnership with Arizona State University to accompany its 30-year collaboration with MIT Press.

Within its pages, authors often reference the complexities of representing process-oriented research in legible ways across interdisciplinary fields, subfields, and specializations. Authors of a 2019 study of articles published between 1974 and 2008 found the editorial focus on interdisciplinarity was a key factor for *Leonardo*'s citational influence. Researchers found that writers of *Leonardo* articles from this 30-year period frequently cite sources from visual art movements known for technological methods and products (kinetic, holographic, cybernetic, computer, and spatial) as well as a wide range of scientific fields with distinct representation from optics, computation, engineering, neuroscience, and psychology. Accordingly, they found a relatively stable trend since the mid-1980s of *Leonardo* articles cited in mainstream science journals such as *Science, Nature*, and *Scientific American* and emerging attention paid in the fields of computer graphics and cognitive science starting in the 1990s (Salah and Leydesdorff 88). The rise of *Leonardo*'s impact within scientific publications by the turn of the twenty-first century appears met with a loss of "citations from [sources in] the art world." The study authors compare this difference in citational patterns to one also observed in the College Art Association's publication, *Art Journal*. A majority of citations of *Art Journal* come from "outside the domain of the arts and the humanities" with the majority from mainstream news media. This study illustrates both the limits of evaluation by category and disciplinary divisions in arts and humanities publications compared to those of the social and natural sciences, and also the "wider cultural influences" of interdisciplinary work that may be less readily embraced in more disciplinary-specific domains (Salah and Leydesdorff 89). There are two types of precarity courted by this kind of disciplinary illegibility. One, encouraged by Yang, where "the whole apparatus of our disciplinary expectations [must] loosen its singular standards of evaluation, but their institutional identities must also be challenged," which could allow

> the possibility of any number of *nth cultures* that do more than simply replicate their own norms indefinitely but instead propose novel, adaptable and robust ones that still lack a complete map. The artist, scientist, writer, philosopher or activist could be one and the same person—and authentically so—working in great uncertainty to redescribe the world in motion.
>
> (320)

The second, less inspirational view of such complexity finds interdisciplinary work relegated to the margins, acknowledged as innovative but without the authority to change systems or structures or singled out as ineffectual because of a unique approach or irreproducibility.

Disciplinary Doubt

The "SciArt" label can describe generalized philosophies of making that trace one origin story back to late 1960s innovations across the arts, the sciences, and technology and the late 1980s emergence of disciplinary hybrids within academia: performance studies, science and technology studies, cultural studies, and medical humanities. While the term shares similar expansiveness as its individual components of "science" and "art," it is also associated with interdisciplinary work within biomedical institutions that fund artists' work that employs the technical tools of laboratory science: the microscope, the centrifuge, the petri dish, incubator, mass spectrometry and spectroscopy, glass and wax models, and so on. There have been a handful of public/privately funded entities in the United Kingdom, Europe, and Australia that support these collaborations, some with a strong public-facing programming and others more focused on opening bench lab spaces to artists. These include the ASCUS Art & Science Lab in Edinburgh, Scotland (2015);[7] Science Gallery London at King's College (2018);[8] Arts at CERN in Switzerland, with its Collide residency (2011);[9] SymbioticA at the University of Western Australia (2000);[10] and

BioArt Lab in Noord Brabant in the Netherlands (2011).[11] In the United States, such spaces are rarer. The Coalesce Center for Biological Art (2016) at the University of Buffalo describes itself as a "hybrid" studio lab run by arts practitioners but seated within the Genome, Environment, and Microbiome (GEM) Community of Excellence.[12] From 2015 to 2020, the SciArt Initiative sponsored the Bridge, a four-month virtual residency, open to international applicants encouraging cross-disciplinary partnerships with a range of possible outcomes.[13] Rensselaer Polytechnic Institute's BioArt Initiative founder, Kathy High, shifted to bio/ecological collaborations, launching the NATURE Lab in 2021 within the Sanctuary for Independent Media in Troy, New York.[14] The School of Visual Arts (SVA) in New York City houses the Bio Art Lab (since 2011) with its summer residency program and offers the reverse construct of a lab, where artists collaborate with the scientific projects in process. This is a biological sciences lab specifically designed for use by artists as part of a bachelor of fine arts program.[15] For now, there are a handful of programs with government-sponsored science agencies such as the Antarctic Artists & Writers Program within the U.S. Antarctic Program sponsored by the National Science Foundation (NSF) and the Artist in Residence at Fermilab America's particle physics and accelerator laboratory.

Within educational circles, one hears the acronym STEAM used to describe interdisciplinarity or, increasingly, collaborative projects are organized around shared matters of concern – perception, cognition, health, presence, interface – instead of disciplinary specialties. Such a structure reflects the dramaturgy of precarity that surrounds education, cultural production, and communication of all knowledge, not just the scientific. Technology has shifted points of access and education from the institution to the individual in ways that make arts training and education seem obsolete. One can shoot, edit, and distribute an entire film with just an iPhone and a handful of apps. These changes, however, affect scientific and technology fields as well. You can learn coding, engineering, and a range of basic sciences via Massive Open Online Courses and other online programs. The conundrum remains about how to best approach training and assessment of interdisciplinarity as the complexity of the worlds in which artists and scientists operate continue to expand. Even a 2018 National Academies of Sciences, Engineering, and Medicine study, "The Integration of the Humanities and Arts with Sciences, Engineering, and Medicine in Higher Education" framed the multiple precarities that surround the teaching, funding, assessment, experimentation, and sustainability of innovative collaborative initiatives as an opportunity:

> Given that today's challenges and opportunities are at once technical and human, addressing them calls for the full range of human knowledge and creativity. Future professionals and citizens need to see when specialized approaches are valuable and when they are limiting, find synergies at the intersections between diverse fields, create and communicate novel solutions, and empathize with the experiences of others.
>
> (8)

Yang offers a similar argument that SciArt research should enjoy generous evaluative metrics because its forges fundamental understandings as the two fields of learning engage each other:

> An epistemic focus on uncertainty seeks a greater engagement with how, why, and with what cultural stakes both science and art are practiced. The value of such work and its impact should be judged on the energy and rigor of the discourse itself and its dispersal through culture more broadly, not whether it contributes to any new discovery in science or appropriately serves in communicating its theories.
>
> (320)

An argument for uncertainty as a metric of value harkens back to the NSF's mission of governmental funding for basic science experimentation, explorations not bound to innovation or immediate productivity to prove their worth. In a similar way, the authors of Future Stage's manifesto argue against performance as commodity but as a "human right," a "human need," providing "the tools of self-actualization, self-esteem, a sense of intimacy, and some social interconnection within communities and among communities" (future-stage.org/). Although these arguments have been somewhat effective in science circles, the financial and cultural investment in artistic experimentation lags behind in ways that technology can both ameliorate and intensify.

"Everything Has a Key"[16]

Is a DJ set music or theater? When the DJ is Paul D. Miller, the answer is yes. And perhaps "set" is too reductive a term for the immersive sonic environments where Miller, as his conceptual art persona DJ Spooky, the Subliminal Kid, is performer, conductor, and creator simultaneously. Miller's interests and products somewhat emulate those of Leonardo, the SciArt's polymath par excellence. In his first monograph, *Rhythm Science* (2004), Miller makes an observation that almost 20 years later seems a statement of fact rather than an act of anticipation: "People are becoming more technological in a way that is at heart how we live and breathe and think in the everyday" (16–17). He notes that the youth of well-resourced countries meet their peers of the global majority living in underresourced places through the common ground of shared technology. Both "come to understand video games, how to use cellphones, and how to navigate their urban and suburban superstructures. They aren't alienated from these technological and geographical phenomena, they are born into them" (17). Technology provides a common ground of experience, consumption, and creation at the same time it illustrates a worrisome dependence on platforms and networks where participants pay for access with their data, such as personal information and consumption habits/patterns without much transparency about its collection and use by whom and for what.

Miller presents "rhythm science" as a strategy to seize the tools and techniques of this digital landscape for creative purposes. Collage, sampling, remix, cut-up, pastiche, found objects/footage, edit, riff, all elements of artmaking that use other art/artists' products now dominate the language and landscape of creation. Miller's early work casts a rather optimistic view of these trends as liberatory. Like sampling, which "uses an endless recontextualizing as a core compositional strategy" (21), rhythm science "builds on the early successes of file-sharing to create a milieu where people can exchange culture and information at will and create new forms, new styles, new ways of thinking" (65). In many ways, Miller's work exemplifies Chemers and Sell's notion of systemic dramaturgy as his worlds are a "collision between code and culture."[17] Musicologist Kate Galloway observes that Miller employs materials deeply embedded within disciplinary research to then set them free via the artistic mix and "collapse either/or binary categories and the gradated hierarchies with which they are intertwined, creating new audience formations and a newly dialectical method for addressing these audiences in the process."

One of these examples is *Terra Nova: Sinfonia Antarctica*, which exists as a performance, a monograph, its own archive of video clips spread across the internet, the open access album *Of Water and Ice* (2013), and the album *Arctic Rhythms* (2014). Miller also continues to tour with Arctic/Antarctic data and evolves its use in his performances as climate change grows more dire. He began building *Terra Nova* when he traveled to Antarctica in 2007 with a portable studio kit collecting "acoustic portraits" of ice as it responded to climate change (Miller, Inside/Out). Its first public performance at the Brooklyn Academy of Music's 2009 New Wave Festival found him mixing his data with that of scientists' "official" findings: "I take data from nature, such as the geometric formulas of snowflakes, and turn them into music," and each trip provides "new information, a new way to relate with the earth, a new language that I can use in my work" (Miller, "Mathematical Musician"). Miller treats the more-than-human world as an archive, similar to the material cultures with which he builds other projects. Such an approach echoes Caridad Svich's notion of all contemporary plays as ecoplays as artists create their work from within a climate crisis reality. Miller takes such association one step further and Galloway notes that his use of the earth as composition material stands in contrast with artists working in the tradition of "ecoconscious music" such as folk, protest songs, even hip-hop where message-driven lyrics are central.

Content as Form as Content

Miller repeated this extended research process with *Heart of the Forest* (2016) a work constructed out of his residencies (each to coincide with a different season) at Oregon State University's Spring Creek Project Long-Term Ecological Reflections program in the H.J. Andrews Experimental Forest.[18] In an approach similar to PearlDamour's *How to Build a Forest*, Miller organizes the work around the passage of time within a forest environment and how the seasons affect an individual's experience of space and place. This research time allowed him to find the forest's "key," which directs the composition's tone and tempo. He mixes material histories into the performance's sonic, visual, and conceptual landscapes, riffing on Vivaldi's *The Four Seasons*, perhaps one of the most canonical classical works eponymous with seasonal change. He invokes the dependence on wood for the fashioning of string instruments, with a symphonic structure that he then interrupts with electronic music crafted from data, archival sources, and drone footage. The specifics of the Andrews forest, its charter member status in the NSF's Long-Term Ecological Research network, its role in early impact studies of forestry in support of logging and in "landscape and water dynamics, carbon sequestration and fluxes, biological diversity, forest-stream interactions" ("History"), all provide Miller with previous transformations to prepare us for the moment when we are no longer present, yet some semblance of the forest remains. Miller offers the audience this experience across time so we might understand the threat to "the lungs of our planet" that sustain human life (Peterson).

In his environmental collaborations, Miller employs the art of the remix to engage scientific data as its skilled interpreter facilitated by technological tools and rendering platforms. He presents a data-informed but not necessarily narrative experience, what Galloway calls "a technopoetics of media activism that intervenes in an ongoing dialectical process" between "the 'natural' and 'manmade' worlds" and their shared traces preserved in ice, water, soil, and animal life. Miller's "sonification" blends sonic registers, visual culture, and live mixing facilitated by technology as one among many languages to render uncertain but dynamic, immersive experiences.[19] He also recognizes music's role in inspiring emotion and the ability to rally people to causes such as environmental activism as well as the preservation of government funding for robust scientific and artistic research:

> You have to have a creative and innovative response. That's just really critical. [The March for Science 2017] is about science, it's about art, it's about music, and about getting rid of all the silos between those mediums and saying hey, people, look, this is all a creative response to a crisis. It's important to try different approaches, and that's what this is about.
>
> (Qtd. in Lawrence)

Such engagement cannot guarantee results. In one of his many recent podcast interviews, Miller speaks less optimistically about the freedom of information and its circulation, noting the influence of what he calls "the furious five" – Apple, Microsoft, Google, Amazon, and Facebook – corporations that collect, analyze, and utilize data to monetize behavioral patterns (Dubber). He laments that ideas like "trend" or "taste" no longer need human action to catalyze an interest or influence; they need only data and a path to production. Yet Miller remains optimistic about artists and the human impulse to create: "Music and art can be vehicles for provoking thought, overcoming inertia, and helping people engage with issues that are exponentially reshaping our information-driven world" (Miller, "Mathematical Musician").

Addressing a Zoom audience in 2021 able to join him in the remote present for a planned lecture hosted by Leeds Beckett University (UK), Miller noted that in this "collision between code and culture," where the attention economy drives the "fourth industrial revolution," the arts have the potential to hold a "free space" for creativity and community as more people are creating than ever before and not just for consumption toward profit. With the pandemic's spike in our dependence on digital resources to connect and conduct daily life, Miller spoke of another possible production focused on how the "planet is humming with human's electrical use," with air, water, even the "axial tilt" of the planet responding to our drives. As much as the pandemic revealed ways that art making illuminates the "possibility of what is possible," the drive for "normalcy above all" seemed destined to reinscribe hollowed-out structures (mined by that furious five) for their familiarity and security. Without a "critical sense of literacy" and a better way to process the "scale" of our actions and their connected effects, Miller expressed concern that we may find ourselves extinct before we can rectify the imbalances we have created. In this worry, Miller shares much common ground with many of the theater artists already discussed.

Theater in Quarantine and the Closet of Curiosities

At the University of Maryland's "Performing Arts in the Digital Age: Interactions and New Directions" symposium in March 2022, Theater in Quarantine (TiQ) presented a short piece developed on-site as part of their selection as the inaugural artists of the Maya Brin Experimental Performance Residency. This was the first time the collaborating artists, Joshua William Gelb and Katie Rose McLaughlin, had worked at the same address since the pandemic began. Their body of work, archived for open and currently free access via their YouTube channel, ranges from two- to three-minute scene studies, test takes, or improvisations with glimpses behind the scenes to more formal productions of 30–40 minutes in length with post-show discussions among collaborators where they share information about inspirations, sources, techniques, and failures with viewers whose chat responses are also visible for those engaging in the moment and after the event (www.youtube.com/c/TheaterinQuarantine). When the Omicron variant postponed the return to in-building performance for many New York theaters in January 2022, TiQ began hosting Digital Salons focused on works in progress and the emerging terrain of digital technology–facilitated theatrical performance.

After showing this excerpt of a new TiQ work to "address the climate crisis" that the artists hope to perform synchronously from all seven continents, Gelb and McLaughlin gave a brief history of TiQ's origins.[20] Mere weeks into the shutdown of in-building work within New York City theaters (April 2020), Gelb was cleaning out a closet in his East Village apartment and discovered, as choreographer McLaughlin described it, "that the aspect ratio of the closet was the same as his phone screen." That discovery became the genesis for the transformation of a 4 x 8 x 2 space into a stage that would house an entire world of performances. Both Gelb and McLaughlin are trained in dance, clowning, and physical theater and boast an impressive list of national and international credentials and collaborations with artists and institutions often invoked when discussing multi-disciplinary, media-forward performance (e.g., Builder's Association, Target Margin Theater, The Tank, and the now-closed Theatre de la Jeune Lune). Neither described themselves as primarily digital artists pre-pandemic, though much of their work has engaged responsive technologies and live-feed video employing software like Isadora and QLab.[21] Living alone, newly confined to one space sparked the pair's desire to dig into the possibilities offered by the remote tools available and to explore the "window into collaboration and community" pandemic-restricted life required.

Starting April 2020, TiQ began producing work, playing with what can be received as "live" by a remote audience. The multiple layers of frame under which the work exists on YouTube often weigh heavily on perception. Audiences only really know the feed is "live" when something fails. In those moments, Gelb opined, "They'll say this is *theater* and that drives me up the wall." He indicated that even when the artists show the Isadora program at work or the sweat pooled on his brow from performing, thus pulling back the curtain on the process, some audience members still insist the work is prerecorded. During their residency, Gelb and McLaughlin explored the relationship among Kinect, QLab, and Isadora (itself created by musician Mark Coniglio) more fully.[22] These are the three motion capture and digital technologies of greatest use in their work with motion tracking providing the greatest integration as a responsive scene partner, allowing the actor freedom from having to synchronize their movements to pre-plotted cues. Once able to work in the same location, TiQ revealed more frames surrounding their performances: the closet space environment wherein a digitally enhanced physical world was rendered, the computer screen doing the rendering with its digital languages, and the in-space audience who could see all renderings at the same time. Even the live stream showed these layers of "the room" and its performance tools. These faded away and reappeared at different points to engage, enhance, or interrupt the flow of action. For TiQ, these revelations provide a key part of the "magic" and knowing the mechanisms open more paths into the experience, complicating every participant's relationship to perception, reality, and story.

"Failure, Isadora, and Walking on the Ceiling"

Many of TiQ's pieces take inspiration from scientific fields – astronautics, oceanography, geography, psychology, virology, computation – as well as the domains where science and art overlap through technologies of representation and record – photography, ethnography, filmmaking, composition, animation, and theater. They report great interest in domains where physical or economic boundaries seem prohibitive for conventional theater – playing with gravity, multiplicity, looping – to discover ways that digital languages expand the universe of possibility. Here, computer capacity (how much it can hold and the expense of hardware and software) meets performer capacity. Gelb is the primary actor; he possesses an impressive array of physical vocabulary matched by an impressive dramaturgical catalog of avant-garde and late-nineteenth-century artistic and historical sources. McLaughlin commented how hard it is for audiences to appreciate Gelb's level of physical exertion. That layer remains somewhat hidden from a YouTube audience; however, post-performance discussions show Gelb sweaty, breathless, and animated in keeping with the long tradition of performers as they meet audience members backstage after a show.

Gelb juggles multiple inputs during performance from the immediate environment to those being synced through the earpiece he wears that cues software and other performers. The reopening of in-building performance offered TiQ a chance to explore new realms of hybridity, adding yet another input of an in-theater audience. In Maryland, TiQ expressed eagerness to find out what this hybridity might mean now that they no longer consider hardware and software as tools but performance languages in and of themselves. With that in mind, the notion of experimentation returns to the forefront of any/all new work that crosses disciplinary boundaries. TiQ's closet "studies" resemble Eadweard Muybridge's nineteenth-century motion studies, some of the earliest unification of art and science to render the temporal plane visible in ways that helped spectators navigate the bridge of perception from real life to life seen through the frame and on the screen. Although the pandemic closed off the typical dimensions of dramaturgy available to theater artists, TiQ adapted and experimented quickly and frequently, essentially treating the dramaturgy of precarity as central force with which to reckon. The conditions of pandemic theater opened a window into process-oriented performance that offered companies an opportunity to build work in full view of a wider public via platforms like YouTube and to uncover new processes, new audiences, and new dramaturgies. How can the willingness to risk and discuss failure become part of the story? TiQ shares a sophistication built from their rehearsal processes that allows them the freedom to follow this kind of question and see where it leads. Their now-archived work on YouTube represents a combination of what was created specifically for the moment, what was done in the moment, and what was improvised because the moment required a change or adaptation. The channel represents perhaps a new iteration of the script anthology, no longer circulating specific stories to be restaged but collecting dramaturgical scores for work that can inspire new pieces using similar or newly discovered vocabularies.

Toward the end of their discussion, TiQ was asked about skill sets for theater students at this moment of seismic shifts exacerbated by the pandemic but also brewing for years prior related to needed changes regarding inclusion, accessibility, and equity across the industry and the discipline. McLaughlin quickly identified "failure," comfortability with failure and the tenacity to transform it. Both mentioned physical theater work, the ability to create and inhabit a world without spoken dialogue. Although devising was not mentioned by name, its horizontally oriented axis of relational tools – physicality, objects, lighting, sound, software, hardware, text – can be seen in TiQ's scene studies. They asserted that their work represents a "tension between extreme analog physicality and the totally digital," and their job as artists is to find ways for these extremes to speak to each other and to audiences in meaningful ways. Certainly proficiencies with Isadora, QLab, and Kinect were reiterated but only alongside or within daily physical theater practice to keep the bodymind at the center of any creative world. As Gelb noted succinctly, "Failure, Isadora, and walking on the ceiling" would be a set of courses in one semester at any "school" of TiQ training. This trio was echoed by the symposium host, multimedia artist Jared Mezzocchi, faculty at the University of Maryland and founder of Virtual Design Collective (ViDCo), who has himself become a champion for a new era of remote, virtual, and digital theater not just as substitute mechanisms used during a global pandemic. Mezzocchi offered "flexible, technical, and uniquely human" as this theater's key principles. In other interviews, he has described the necessity for theater to "examine human behavior within technological landscapes" (Kaan). Although hardware and software can facilitate our connections, Mezzocchi and artists like TiQ represent how technology might bring new dramaturgies of precarity to the storytelling table.

Enduring Matters of Concern

These examples represent technology-generative over technology-facilitated work. Although there is an undeniable dominance of visual tools and products, embodiment (whether performer, audience, or an interplay between them) remains central, even if spoken or written text does not. Again, as in other interdisciplinary work, ruminations on temporality, interdependence, and precarity find collaborative partners in science and technology to address climate change, environmental degradation, and health/mortality. The artists' work discussed represent what Barbara Maria Stafford calls "contemporary ineffabilities," those domains of life that "ordinary, intelligent people cannot find words for," ones facilitated in new ways by digital technologies but having enticed artists and scientists for hundreds of years (8). Technology also facilitates portable engagements that can exceed and extend an on-stage performance experience such as *Ocean Filibuster*'s augmented reality app, *Deep Wonder*'s and *Rollover*'s proposed virtual reality experience, *Shelter in Place.* The Works on Water's installations integrated *(Not) Water*'s imaginative world into other artists' conceptualization of climate change impacts some that used video, time-lapse photography, audio-facilitated site tours, and digital repositories of stories and remixed data. Project/artist websites provide an archival chronicle of process and a real-time repository of research news and information even as all navigate ongoing issues related to storage, obsolescence, and even malfeasance by other digital actors. Streaming technology and adaptations of script/performance for remote interface allowed me access to a version of *SPILL*'s performance script and to experience *Frozen Fluid, The Catastrophist,* and *Ocean Filibuster* when on-site attendance was impossible due to the pandemic. These are more conventional uses of technology as tool, but they also represent interdisciplinary spaces and practices where the role of world building expands beyond writer, script, and theater stage, pressing the formal and experiential dimensions of story and storytelling. They also have the potential to become more closely enmeshed as at the S.T.A.G.E. Collaboratory but only with significant investment in the cultural and education sectors beyond philanthropic or commercial engines.

In 2018, the John S. and James S. Knight Foundation's Prototype Fund announced awards ($50,000) for 12 projects "to help the cultural sector adapt and thrive in the digital age." First-round funds were application based, literally. They were mobile apps, virtual reality, and remote connectivity tools to provide broader access for patrons and software for data analytics of attendance, revenue, and future planning. The next year, Knight joined with the Ford Foundation to help the National Endowment for the Arts (NEA) pursue a "field scan" (2019–2021) of artists "who use technology as a creative medium," a broad umbrella term to include as many cultural sector domains and individuals as possible (Ball). The report findings illustrate the tenacity of "tech-centered" artists to find collaborators, innovators, and audiences in "virtual and physical spaces" despite the difficulty of securing funding because the assessment of these artists, their processes, and their products remain abstruse to traditional arts and science grantors, institutions, and reviewers. Report editor Don Ball noted how higher education spaces provide critical funding of laboratories for this work, though the general precarity of arts/humanities programs within said institutions went unremarked. Commissioned prior to the COVID-19 pandemic, the catastrophic changes to the performing arts field and industry wrought by global disruptions shifted previously incremental digital integrations into high gear but often without staff, financial, or even aesthetic infrastructure to guide choices that might be dictated by survival first and foremost. Many established theater companies did not survive the pandemic, but as can be seen with TiQ, new companies have been forged. The question remains as to how the industry and the discipline will recalibrate their processes and practices in response given another shared value between the arts and the sciences: the desire for a sure thing. It took until 2019 for the NEA to conduct a significant study of the status of "tech-centered" U.S. artists. COVID-19 pandemic disruptions have not been met with a robust restructuring of government funding priorities (universal basic income, universal health care, universal education) or a dismantling of the monopolies held by Miller's furious five and their compatriots. Against such a backdrop, the pages of *Leonardo* might continue to represent the unique, groundbreaking, and experimental for only a niche circle of awareness, with the potential collaborators and the larger public denied the robust interdisciplinary experience of experimentation that Frank Malina imagined.

Notes

1 These questions echo aspects of Djerassi's critique of the use of "science" as a modifier for the wide range of artistic products made by those without scientific education/experience even as he established the Djerassi Resident Artist Program in 1979 to host an array of interdisciplinary creators.
2 Shepherd-Barr anticipates the question of whether "stage machinery and engineering … are actually forms of 'science'" or if broadening that term to include these, as well as theatrical labor, renders it "meaningless by being too diffuse" (217).
3 See, for example, Yeo and McKasy.
4 See Coren and Safer for one example.
5 The SciArt Initiative, founded in 2014 by artist Julia Buntaine Hoel, has created intriguing and open access digital content, including a *SciArt Magazine*. I chose to focus on *Leonardo* given its longevity and peer-review structure.
6 In his prodigious body of work exploring the relationship between art and science practice and theory from the Renaissance to the postmodern age, British art historian Martin Kemp has over fifty publications devoted to da Vinci's work as artist, scientist, and engineer.
7 ascus.org.uk/ascus-lab/.
8 london.sciencegallery.com/.
9 arts.cern/.
10 symbiotica.uwa.edu.au/.
11 bioartlab.com/.
12 buffalo.edu/genomeenvironmentmicrobiome/coalesce.html.
13 sciartinitiative.org/the-bridge.html.
14 mediasanctuary.org/initiatives/nature-lab/.
15 bioart.sva.edu.
16 Miller uses this phrase in a promotional video for his "Heart of a Forest" project.
17 Miller used this phrasing in his April 28, 2021 Inside/Out remote lecture at Leeds Beckett University (UK) and at an April 17, 2017 podcast taping at the Carnegie Institution for Science (qtd. in Galloway).
18 Established in 2003 with plans to exist until 2303, the Spring Creek Project describes its mission as one "to bring together writers, humanists, and scientists to create a living, growing record of how we understand the forest and the relation of people to the forest, as that understanding and that forest both change over time" (liberalarts.oregonstate.edu/centers-and-initiatives/spring-creek-project/programs-and-residencies/long-term-ecological-reflections).
19 The dominance of this form and collaborations is reflected in the 30-year run (1991–2021) of the *Leonardo Music Journal*, which chronicled the "aesthetic and technical issues in contemporary music and the sonic arts" ("Thirty Years of Leonardo Music Journal").
20 All direct quotes from Gelb or McLaughlin are from this March 11, 2022 symposium discussion.
21 Not many theater productions in the twenty-first century can do without these tools even when running basic lighting and sound cues.

22 In a 2002 interview with Scott deLahunta, Coniglio was asked whether Isadora itself should be considered a work of art. He said no, but it bears the marks of his design and its modes of functionality were built out of collaborations with artists in anticipation of their uses.

References

Ball, Don, editor. "Tech as Art: Supporting Artists Who Use Technology as a Creative Medium." *National Endowment for the Arts*, 2021. arts.gov/impact/research/publications/tech-art-supporting-artists-who-use-technology-creative-medium.

Chemers, Michael, and Michael Sell. "*Sokyokuchi*: Toward a Theory, History, and Practice of Systemic Dramaturgy." *Theatre History Studies*, vol. 39, 2020, pp. 24–52. doi:10.1353/ths.2020.0002.

Coren, Emily, and Devra Safer. "Storytelling and GIS Accelerating Climate Solutions." *American Geophysical Union*, 8 Dec. 2020. Conference Paper. Vimeo. vimeo.com/482351974.

"Dejerassi's Legacy to the Arts." *Punch Magazine: Spirit of the Peninsula*, 1 Sept. 2018. punchmagazine.com/djerassis-legacy-to-the-arts/.

deLahunta, Scott. "Isadora 'Almost Out of Beta': Tracing the Development of a New Software Tool for Artists." *Software for Dancers: The User's Guide*, 15 Sept. 2002. sdela.dds.nl/sfd/isadora.html.

Dixon, Steve. *A History of New Media in Theater, Dance, Performance Art, and Installation*. MIT Press, 2007. doi:10.7551/mitpress/2429.001.0001.

Dubber, Andrew, host. "Episode 27, Paul D. Miller – DJ Spooky." *Music Tech Fest*, mtflabs.net/podcast027/.

Future Stage Research Group. "Future Stage Manifesto." metaLAB Harvard, 25 Oct. 2021. future-stage.org/.

Galloway, Kate. "Remixing the Environment: Climate Change, Rhythm Science, and DJ Spooky's Digging in the Landscape." *The Oxford Handbook of Hip Hop Music*, edited by Justin D. Burton and Jason Lee Oakes, Oxford University Press, 2018. doi:10.1093/oxfordhb/9780190281090.013.19.

Gelb, Joshua William. "About." www.joshuawilliamgelb.com/about.

Glueck, Grace. "Scientist Brings Art to His Work: Billy Kluver's Skill Goes into Friends' Creations." *New York Times*, 17 Dec. 1965. https://www.proquest.com/historical-newspapers/scientist-brings-his-art-his-work/docview/117083240/se-2?accountid=10598.

"History." HJ Andrews Experimental Forest LTER. 2011–2022. andrewsforest.oregonstate.edu/about/history.

Kaan, Gil. "Jared Mezzocchi's Guided Tour Thru His & Someone Else's House." *Broadway World*, 30 Apr. 2021. http://www.broadwayworld.com/los-angeles/article/BWW-Interview-Jared-Mezzocchis-Guided-Tour-Thru-His-SOMEONE-ELSES-HOUSE-20210430..

"Knight Prototype Fund Awards $600,000 to 12 Projects that Explore Avenues for Connecting People with the Arts through Technology." Knight

Foundation, 12 July 2018. knightfoundation.org/press/releases/knight-prototype-fund-awards-projects-that-explore-avenues-for-connecting-people-with-the-arts-through-tech/.

La Mont, Pierre. "'A Pretty Wild Idea': Interview with Roger Malina." *Medium*, 17 Oct. 2017. medium.com/@OfficialCLM/a-pretty-wild-idea-899b6a6e046f.

Latour, Bruno. *Spinoza Lectures: What Is the Style of Matters of Concern?* VanGorcum, 2005.

Lawrence, Michael. "DJ Spooky Explains How Sound Shapes Our Understanding of Politics." *VICE*, 24 Mar. 2017. vice.com/en/article/yp9baj/dj-spooky-intercepted-interview.

Lehmann, Hans-Thies, and Patrick Primavesi. "Dramaturgy on Shifting Grounds." *Performance Research*, vol. 14, no. 3, 2010, pp. 3–6.

McLaughlin, Katie Rose, Artistic Director. *Designated Movement Company.* designatedmovement.org/katie-rose-mclaughlin/.

Miller, Paul D. "A Mathematical Musician's Journey from Our Nation's Capital to the Arctic Circle." *Our Arctic Nation. Special Edition of Medium*, 13 May 2016. medium.com/our-arctic-nation/week-19-washington-dc-e1c8677d9faa.

Miller, Paul D. "Heart of a Forest" promotional page. djspooky.com/heart-of-a-forest/.

Miller, Paul D. Inside/Out lecture at Leeds Beckett University. *Zoom*, 28 Apr. 2021.

Miller, Paul D. *Rhythm Science.* MIT Press, 2004.

Miller, Paul D. "Terra Nova: Sinfonia Antarctica" promotional page. djspooky.com/terra-nova-sinfonia-antarctica/.

National Academies of Sciences, Engineering, and Medicine. "The Integration of the Humanities and Arts with Sciences, Engineering, and Medicine in Higher Education: Branches from the Same Tree." The National Academies Press, 2018. doi:10.17226/24988.

Pendle, George. "Leonardo's Strange Angel: Behind the Scenes with Jack Parsons and Frank Malina." *Leonardo Blog*, 11 Jun. 2018, leonardo.info/blog/2018/06/12/leonardos-strange-angel.

Peterson, Isaac. "A Convergence of Art and Science: An Interview with DJ Spooky." *1859 Oregon Magazine*, 3 Mar. 2017. 1859oregonmagazine.com/live/music/dj-spooky/.

Salah, Alkim Almila Akdag, and Loet Leydesdorff. "The Development of the Journal Environment of Leonardo." *Leonardo*, vol. 45, no. 1, 2012, pp. 88–89. www.jstor.org/stable/41421812.

Shepherd-Barr, Kirsten E. "'The Stage Hand's Lament': Scenography, Technology, and Off-Stage Labour." *The Cambridge Companion to Theatre and Science*, edited by Kirsten E. Shepherd-Barr, Cambridge University Press, 2020, pp. 203–218.

Stafford, Barbara Maria. "On Being Struck: Hitting the Eye/Arousing the Mind." *Ribbon of Darkness: Inferencing from the Shadowy Arts and*

Sciences. University of Chicago Press, 2019, pp. 1–12. doi:10.7208/chicago/9780226630656.001.0001.

"University of Maryland Symposium: Performing Arts in the Digital Age, Interactions and New Directions. Performance and Workshop by Theater in Quarantine (TiQ)." *HowlRound*, 11 Mar. 2022. howlround.com/happenings/livestreaming-performance-and-workshop-theatre-quarantine-tiq.

Theater in Quarantine. *YouTube*. youtube.com/c/TheaterinQuarantine.

"Thirty Years of Leonardo Music Journal: Conversation with Erica Hruby." 15 Oct. 2020. mitpress.mit.edu/thirty-years-of-leonardo-music-journal/.

Yang, Andrew. "That Drunken Conversation Between Two Cultures: Art, Science and the Possibility of Meaningful Uncertainty." *Leonardo*, vol. 48, no. 3, 2015, pp. 318–321. doi:10.1162/LEON_a_00705.

Yeo, Sara K., and Meaghan McKasy. "Emotion and Humor as Misinformation Antidotes." *Proceedings of the National Academy of Sciences of the United States of America*, vol. 118, no. 15, 2021. doi:10.1073/pnas.2002484118.

5 Dramaturgy of Care

The Medical Landscape of Science Theater

When a recent group of my *Performing Science* students expressed dismay that a play for young audiences about famous women in science omitted the details of a historical character's medical education from its plot, I asked them, "What *science* is *medicine*?" The room grew quiet. One student offered, "All the life sciences." Another chimed in, "Plus the physical sciences." "And math." "Statistics and computer science," added others. With such a list, we agreed that representing all the scientific fields a medical student might encounter would overwhelm the play. Then one student speculated, "Maybe the playwright focuses on the time after the character becomes a doctor because medicine is the science of human beings."[1] It seemed a fitting compromise as when medicine does appear in plays, the predominant focus is on patients' struggle with illness and their conflicts with institutions and individuals (mostly physicians) that either provide them with needed treatment or limit their access and ignore or exacerbate their suffering. Many science play compendiums include titles that depict the physician, geneticist, or other medical researcher from Molière's *The Imaginary Invalid* and Shaw's *The Doctor's Dilemma* to Edward Albee's *Who's Afraid of Virginia Woolf*, Jonathan Tolins's *The Twilight of the Golds* and Tony Kushner's *Angels in America*. Djerassi singled out theater scholars' inclusion of medicine's expanse of topics and techniques in his critique of overly broad designations of "science plays,"[2] and yet to omit medicine (its pedagogy, practice, and research) from a dramaturgical analysis of U.S. science theater in the twenty-first century seems imprudent.

Perhaps the most famous example of a medicine-centered science play of the past 25 years is Margaret Edson's 1999 Pulitzer Prize–winning *W;t*. The action follows English professor Vivian Bearing and

DOI: 10.4324/9781003150848-6

her grueling and ultimately unsuccessful experimental treatment for ovarian cancer, which unfolds as we share her last hours of life punctuated by flashbacks to her childhood, teaching career, and diagnosis. Edson depicts the humbling and often humiliating journey toward death within Western biomedicine by having her protagonist speak to the audience in direct address, translating her evolving experience and understanding of suffering through explicating John Donne's exquisite but dense texts. We see Bearing's cold and uncompromising classroom demeanor, and it is unpleasantly similar to how she is treated by the care team save for her nurse, Susie. A domineering force in academia, in the hospital Bearing experiences the total authority of medicine. Her cancer treatments are depicted or described in excruciating detail. For all the abstractions of metaphysical poetry, the multiple productions I have seen and reviews I have read highlight the physical demands on the actor playing Bearing, especially the final moments of the play where she experiences a punishing CPR code.

W;t arrived Off-Broadway in 1998 and ran for two years and over 500 performances. It also made an indelible imprint on medical school education through the *W;t* Educational Initiative (WEI; 2000–2002) and the *W;t* Film Project (2002–2004) created by doctors at the David Geffen School of Medicine[3] at UCLA (Sweet). Both of these initiatives had a similar goal: "using the dramatic arts to improve medical education in end-of-life care" by presenting a full theatrical production or a reading of *W;t* or a screening of its HBO film version to medical students and house staff followed by facilitated discussions, providing "a 'safe haven' for attendees to express their strong feelings related to caring for dying patients" (Lorenz et al. 483). This work was part of a self-critique at the turn of the twenty-first century that found "medical education has come to emphasize a biomedical rather than holistic model of illness," and when it came to a patient's end of life, physicians so trained were ill-equipped to address the "psychological, social, and spiritual dimensions of illness" (481). Of particular import to the WEI founders was the opportunity for the play to serve as an alternative to "traditional didactic" approaches of end-of-life pedagogy, to "show versus tell" about patient experiences (481). Similar to the supporting expert talks and symposia around *Copenhagen* and *Proof* mentioned in chapter 1, WEI represents another example of a popular science play capturing a "two cultures" zeitgeist that invites their collaboration. *W;t* offered an emotionally compelling, relatively portable, and pedagogically inclined object to school of medicine faculty who might have recognized themselves or their students in its physician characters. Or they might have recognized an emerging public relations crisis as viewers and critics empathized with the suffering of the play's main character.

WEI was a well-intentioned, well-organized, and necessary step toward including embodied, experiential learning in medical education. Its limits reside in an emphasis on a theater script over the embodied experiences available in/around a script's production and a focus on expanding medical professionals' capacity for empathy versus challenging their authority over bodily experience by engaging with subjects who respond and resist. This chapter addresses these limits by exploring theater's appearance within medical domains as a story and teaching tool, examining the field and practices of narrative medicine and the use of plays to inform and engage clinicians and pre-health students whose core conceptualizations of health and healing is shaped by STEM-oriented knowledge and practices devoted to cure. By way of contrast, the chapter also takes up **dramaturgies of care** emerging from theater artists who shift theater's use in medicine away from script analysis, development, and performance toward embodied research informed by medical discourse. To that end, the work of Marina Tsaplina and Anne Basting serve as examples of how artists might position themselves as researchers sometimes alongside, sometimes in challenge to the medical establishment, disrupting notions of unitary autonomy and authority, providing strategies for creative research so that theater practitioners and medical personnel might fruitfully engage principles of health justice and equity across the "two cultures."

Empathy as Experience

Before Rita Charon (internal medicine M.D. and English literature Ph.D.) drafted her foundational arguments for narrative medicine as its own academic field, the arts in health movement of the late 1970s/early 1980s found medical professionals, caregivers, and patients crafting text-based narratives (poetry, short stories, novels, essays, and plays) to chronicle their experiences in medicine. Poetry publications and an array of writing programs for patient-authors and physician-authors within teaching hospitals were organized alongside other arts initiatives within hospital spaces with a focus on music and visual art. Researchers began studying expressive writing's therapeutic value, and that work combined with the postmodern era of literary theory and its "questioning of certainty and the realizations of language's ever shifting representations of reality" made narrative, in Charon's view, a fertile clinical ground where collaboration and contestation over meaning was necessary to understand the fullness of the human condition especially in extremis (Charon et al. 1).[4]

In a 2001 article that outlines the initial trajectories of narrative medicine, Charon asserts that "medicine practiced with narrative competence," produced through "close reading of literature and reflective writing," allows "physicians to reach and join their patients in illness, recognize their own personal journeys through medicine, acknowledge kinship with and duties towards other healthcare professionals, and inaugurate consequential discourse with the public about healthcare" (Charon 1897). Almost two decades later in the first clinical guide to the field, *Principles and Practice of Narrative Medicine* (2017), Charon and her coauthors describe the process of reading as shared and embodied, "an ethical act joining reader and writer in transformative engagement" (Charon et al. 1). They define "text" expansively: "fiction, poem, play, visual image, or musical composition" (183). The classroom examples they feature, however, are predominantly poems or excerpts from novels. *W;t* is the exception, but even when discussed in a chapter exploring phenomenology, the embodied component of the play's staging goes unmentioned in favor of quoting Bearing's lines about her diagnosis and treatment.[5] Even in her 2001 article, however, Charon invokes competencies relevant to theater as she describes the role that health-care professionals play in a medical drama: "Listening to stories of illness and recognizing that there are often no clear answers to patients' narrative questions demand the courage and generosity to tolerate and bear witness to unfair losses and random tragedies" (Charon 1899). Neuroscientist Alice Flaherty, who undertook the role of a standardized patient to better understand the ways performance training might shape empathetic communication, more directly asserts the research contributions theatrical performance can make to medicine and vice versa: "Such analyses might help doctors and patients realize that acting skills are crucial for their communication, and theatrical actors learn more about how their bodies generate emotional behavior" (11).

Such ideas illuminate another limitation of medicine's engagement with/employment of theatrical texts: the focus on building health-care professionals' empathetic capacities. In the early days of the arts in health care movement, the arts' purpose was to bring expression and comfort to patients, caregivers, and personnel. In his preface to the 1991 *Hospital Arts Handbook* edited by Janice Palmer and Florence Nash, Duke University Medical Center physician Dr. James Semans prescribes the arts as a "healthy distraction … from the premonition and preoccupation which the unknown brings to an ill person."[6] The arts provide transcendence in ways that exceed the physician's capacity, but because physicians "care about the feelings of patients," Semans argues, they should take specific actions to facilitate arts access (2). In 2001, Dr. Charon includes the physician in this loop, insisting that self-care and emotion are key competencies of practice:

> Accomplishing such acts of witnessing allows the physician to proceed to his or her more recognizably clinical narrative tasks: to establish a therapeutic alliance, to generate and proceed through a differential diagnosis, to interpret physical findings and laboratory reports correctly, to experience and convey empathy for the patient's experience, and, as a result of all these, to engage the patient in obtaining effective care.
>
> (Charon 1899)

And in 2019, *Wall Street Journal* reporter Sumathi Reddy profiles an array of hospital-based narrative medicine programs, from creative writing workshops for staff and patients to physicians reading poetry to and with patients. She describes these offerings as innovative but raises questions about cost, assessment, and scalability.[7] Reddy also highlights a new aspect of the ongoing efforts to imbue the clinical encounter with empathy: the hope that narrative medicine and other arts in health approaches have "the potential to alleviate doctor burnout," a named crisis within health-care circles since 2015 when over 46% of American Medical Association–surveyed physicians reported feeling its symptoms.[8]

Additional studies of health-care workers have found an urgent need to address "moral injury," conditions exacerbated by health-care systems where corporatized interests reduce time and human resources in the name of efficiency.[9] Empathy is often invoked by practitioners and critics alike as one of theater's strongest experiential outcomes toward building relational capacity. In their 2005 keynote to the Mid-Atlantic Theater Conference, "The Uses of Empathy: Theater and the Real World," writers/activists Jessica Blank and Erik Jenson argue that narrative theater "triggers identifications [that] crack open our comfortable, sedimented everyday identities and generate reactions and questions," offering us an opportunity to connect:

> When we empathize, the wall between self and other, between us and them, begins to disintegrate. We can no longer view the other as an abstraction or an object—we have to experience the other as

> human; as human as ourselves. And then the questions that their stories raise … become our questions too.
>
> (19)

Certainly, the starting point for action must include conceptualizations of self and other in relationship, but psychologist Paul Bloom, among others, have argued empathy's focus on the individual remains an enduring problem, making it a less effective resource to answer systemic injustices (Bloom 34–35).[10]

Narrative medicine's overemphasis on empathy can be matched with skepticism regarding its emphasis on so-called great texts in the Western canon, many that reinforce a medical model of illness and disability. A reader or audience member might gain insight from the struggles of characters depicted, but the perspective risks being steeped in ableism, suffering, and tragedy. The history of representation within medical research and education as well as theater stages and play anthologies often seems bereft of vitality and pleasure experienced by those who are ill or disabled. An example of the use-value limits on theatrical empathy can be found in geneticists Karen Rothenberg and Lynn Bush's 2012 article for the *Houston Journal of Health Law & Policy*, "Manipulating Fate: Medical Innovations, Ethical Implications, Theatrical Illuminations." The authors chronicle 46 plays from the nineteenth- to twenty-first centuries, a list that includes several Sloan commissions, *W;t*, and the medicine cum science play titles cited at the start of this chapter. They assert that these texts illustrate "attempts to manipulate fate by advances in medical science" (5) in ways that "generate fear, create hope, transform identity, and inspire empathy" (4) and offer readers a chance to "reflect the role that legal and bioethical principles can play to mediate these tensions in society" (3). Their examples abound with altruistic physicians-researchers who "thirst to increase their knowledge of disease processes," which in turn "fuels their fortitude to strive for the betterment of the patient" (32). In the majority of their examples, characters experience unwelcome and unpleasant conditions and seek medical intervention, often unsuccessfully. And while such examples demonstrate how "theatre highlights the very real drama faced by many in society when cures, treatments, and palliative care are lacking" (49), Rothenberg and Bush focus on "the promise of science to move forward" and the role of theater to "encourag[e] the creation of innovation and protect … the public from ineffective interventions" (70). They include themselves as those encouraged to find "medical innovations to manipulate [human] fate" (7), but their selected texts neglect any alternative understandings of and attitudes toward medicine, illness, and disability. Even characters who accept their "fate" do so while longing to be alleviated of their burdensom conditions.

Moving from Cure to Care

Dramatic texts that focus on the conflicts and crises that accompany mortality, illness, and disability reflect the tales that also dominate news outlets, so often told from the perspective of those adjacent to the experience (caregivers, physicians) who in telling their own stories cannot help but speak for others. Narrative theater tends to follow a protagonist's pursuit of desires, someone who encounters and overcomes obstacles and as such is primed to depict illness and disability as limitations. It reinforces social dynamics expressed in stories of the individual who "refuses to let [insert chronic condition here] stop him from achieving his dreams." As poet-scholar Eli Clare observes, "in a world that places extraordinary value in cure, the belief that we can defeat or transcend body-mind conditions through individual hard work is convenient. Overcoming is cure's back-up plan" (10). Clare dissects the "ideology of cure" that envelopes medicine as a discipline, a practice, and an industry. Affirming his own reliance on the tools and products of medical research, Clare rejects the control and definition such reliance demands of those who need it:

> Cure saves lives and ends lives, propels eradication and promises us that our body-minds can change. It is a tool in the drive to normalize humans, to shrink the diversity of shape, form, size and function among us. Through cure, we believe we can control our fragile, changeable, adaptable selves.
>
> (70)

Similarly, medical anthropologist Annamarie Mol scrutinizes the "logic of choice," a neoliberal ideal wherein a patient exerts her "control" over long- or short-term illness conditions by becoming a consumer of medicine's products and programs (1). Not only does such a logic presuppose patients possess agency and capacity, but it also implies that discernment is as easy as information gathering and decision-making. Mol blends cure with care, noting that for many with chronic conditions, cure is less about a recovery that medicine enables and more about medicine making "life more bearable: it is a form of care" (7). For her, a fundamental principle of a logic of care is that it "contain[s] more suitable repertoires for handling life with a disease" because it asserts the "fleshliness and fragility of life" in both its tedium and extremis: "The logic of care is not preoccupied with our will, and with what we may opt for, but concentrates on what we do" (8–9). Thus, dramaturgies of care emphasize building capacity for action.

Some of that action has already brought change. Over the past 20 years, there has been an eightfold growth in medical and health humanities programs in the United States and Canada. This upward trajectory exists at a time when humanities majors are declining even within elite liberal arts institutions (Lamb, Berry, and Jones). There is no singular reason behind the growth. At some institutions, these programs are the culmination of many years of advocacy on the part of students and faculty; at others, they are a strategic interdisciplinary collaboration in response to budget cuts and student demand, including a revised MCAT that places more emphasis on social determinants of health.[11] There is not yet a corresponding growth of stand-alone disability studies programs;[12] however, many of the newest curricula use health humanities instead of medical humanities as public discourse regarding the physician as singular authority over care has shifted to recognize a host of entities with biomedical knowledge and economic influence over access to health care, including professions that "exceed the biomedical" especially in the rapidly expanding "wellness" industry (Epstein and Timmermans 244). This shift also reflects a growing value within medical education of interdisciplinary inquiry coupled with interprofessional competencies across care teams (nursing, physical therapy, occupational therapy, public health) and acknowledges medicine's social contexts, an awareness that health (and illness) is determined by many more factors than just medical intervention or affirmation (Crawford et al. 1–19). In this way, while not yet directly addressing disability studies and disability justice, these new programs and initiatives are spaces wherein "disability literacy" might find purchase as health professions students become more aware of the worlds in which they will operate – in the words of G. Thomas Couser, "where theory meets practice, where thinking about human variation is powerfully brought to bear on bodies and minds at risk" (29). These are the pedagogical contexts that surround the artistic research of Marina Tsaplina (embodiment and puppetry [E&P]) and Anne Basting (creative care). The rest of this chapter explores their curricular practices and products as these provide an opportunity to explore and craft dramaturgies of care within healthcare spaces, places where, in Mol's words, professionals aspire "to serve the good life while attending to a reality of erratic, fleshly, mortal bodies" (15).

The Tremble

Tsaplina's directive sounds simple: *Keep your feet planted on the ground, feel the connection with the earth. Look at the feather in your one hand and try to keep it from moving. Hold it still without tightening your grip, intervening with your other hand, or resting it against something for stability.*[13] The students in this visual cultures of medicine class previously seated around a seminar table with laptops and notebooks at the ready now find themselves standing, breathing deeply, each holding a wire and fabric feather navigating what Tsaplina calls the "inner tremble." The tremble is our body's innate expression of being alive in ways that exceed, even resist, our conscious control. It takes a while to settle into an alternative stance in the room, and there are furtive glances as the students survey their peers to see strategies, successes, failures. *Notice if you took steps, like holding your breath, to try and bring the feather under control.* The students smile and some nod in recognition. *Did you hold your breath in search of stillness, and did that tension make the tremble even more pronounced?* More nods, some sheepish grins, and a few still turn the object and their bodies this way and that to see if they can find the trick to achieve the goal.

Tsaplina concretizes this metaphor because the idea of bodily control threads through medical education in fundamental ways. Such control is, as Clare notes, another expression of the ideology of cure, which "grounds itself in an original state of being, relying on a belief that what existed before is superior to what exists currently. And … it seeks to return what is damaged to that former state of being" (15). For Tsaplina and Clare, both who navigate chronic conditions that preclude any "return" to perfect health, this disconnect influences all aspects of medical science from the clinical encounter to the funding of research. In Clare's words:

> The vision of me without tremoring hands and slurred speech, with more balance and coordination, doesn't originate from my visceral history. Rather it arises from an imagination of what I should be like, from some definition of *normal* and *natural*.
>
> (15)

Although most of the pre-health students in this class are familiar with representational arts and narrative performances that depict the lived experience of illness, the feather exercise asks them to focus a bit closer to home for how precarity resides actively within not at some anticipated time but right now. Tsaplina presents puppetry/object theater as an opportunity for experiential experiments to inspire would-be health-care practitioners' imaginations, once steeped in cure, to open to the complex and relational practices of care.

Imaginative Practices of Care

I met Tsaplina in 2016 when we were part of a cohort of six Kienle scholars in medical humanities at Penn State College of Medicine. Performing artist, patient advocate, and medical humanities scholar, at the time her primary role was founder and CEO of The Betes, a nonprofit organization (2013–2018) comprised of patients, caregivers, and clinicians using theater to articulate lived experiences of diabetes, the "betes" of the organization's name.[14] One of her first Betes puppet forms consisted of a blue surgical glove worn on her hand with two buttons from her shirt for its eyes. A more refined version of this entity became the "face" of The Betes brand, but more important for Tsaplina, it served as a "body-pen" to articulate her experiences and to offer others the same: "The puppet was a means of embodying this tension of the *it-and-me* of my illness, … a body that helped this mutual articulation to take place at all – akin to how the microscope opens access to our cells" (Tsaplina, "Bodies Speaking" 90). Tsaplina searched for ways to rewrite medicine's "definitive finalized statement about this state of being of a body" as she developed her first quasi-narrative pieces: *The Overneath* and *The Invisible Elephant Project*. Externalizing her disability through puppetry demanded that she "open a new articulation and be able to enter the mystery of its presence, … to release the name [diabetes] and its associations." What emerged was an understanding of the illness as "wild, untamable, and fundamentally strange" (Tsaplina, "Bodies Speaking" 91). Such a process was facilitated by Tsaplina's training as a puppetry artist who understands the artistic form as not just epistemological, concerned with knowledge that can be represented and measured, but as ontological, concerned with states of being that are often multiple realities at the same time:

> By articulating "diabetes" through the practice of physical theatre, a new *diabetes* emerges. This *diabetes* is not entirely separate from the one that is enacted through biotechnology, yet it is not the same. It is more than singular, but less than many.
>
> (Tsaplina, "Bodies Speaking" 92)

Her reading of her diabetes through the lens of physical theater recalls Brecht's alienation effect: "a representation … which allows us to recognize its subject, but at the same time makes it seem unfamiliar" (Brecht 192). This is a complicated duality to ask of artists, let alone clinicians who may have only considered the idea of performance and representation in medicine when being evaluated for their work with standardized patients, or encountering narrative medicine methods or expressive writing workshops, or when exposed to plays or films (e.g., the WEI).

Like Florida-based Mickee Faust theater's "Ethics of Accommodation"[15] and St. Louis's Uppity Theatre Company's "access aesthetics,"[16] Tsaplina's E&P curriculum for pre-health and medical students shifts the focus away from audience reception to participant interactivity. She provides would-be clinicians with an individualized sensory experience, recognizing that a domain largely left unexamined for the physician in training is the sensory attunement of their own bodyminds. Medical institutions have engaged actors for many years in standardized patient curricula, have encouraged acting or improvisation classes for physicians in training, particularly geared toward providing awareness of social cues, vocal modulation, development of bedside manner and improvisation toward expressions of empathy, and most recently, encouraging self-care programs, including yoga and meditation.[17] Tsaplina's practice centers stillness and breath and offers students an opportunity to work poetically with their own body-pens. She employs disability as a lens for the analysis of medicine rather than building representational performances based on first-person experiences and conveying those stories to health-care professionals in hopes they will carry remembered empathy into their clinical practice. For Tsaplina, such an approach tends to present patients as passive recipients of a kindly physician's actions or to focus on an individual's fortitude in overcoming social and medical barriers rather than "notice how the world needs to change to become inclusive to disability" (Tsaplina, "Puppetry and Disability Aesthetics").

In contrast, Tsaplina's E&P curriculum provides students with analytical vocabulary drawn from phenomenology and anthropology alongside puppet and physical theater so they might consider the idea of "plural bodies," how even in our singular bodymind we are the product of multiple forces.[18] The notion of plurality undergirds a few key principles of her curriculum. First, inviting participants to animate figures that do not mimic "disability" in stereotypical ways (Tsaplina, Odendahl-James, and Bend 17). Such nonrepresentational work keeps attention focused on elemental questions about being and relationship. Second, moving participants beyond naturalism and objectification when engaging a puppet figure that is atypical allows them to interrogate what atypical means and for whom because "the very material of a puppet body/performing object creates an opportunity to cross normative borders the way few mediums can" (Tsaplina, "Puppetry and Disability Aesthetics"). Third, that everyone involved works to "mind the gap" between "what you think you know about disability and what disability communities are saying" (Tsaplina, "Puppetry and Disability Aesthetics"). This means Tsaplina provides only one of many lived experiences of disability for the curriculum, which continues to develop with the contributions of participants and consultants authorized to disrupt any self-confirming circles of representation and experiment with techniques to rewire the medical imagination.

Writing about the possibilities of imagination in the health humanities with physician Raymond Barfield, Tsaplina invokes recent research of cognitive science that supports theater and performance studies' long-held notion of embodiment as epistemology: "'Natural cognitive systems … participate in the generation of meaning through their bodies and action… . They enact a world.' [This] 'enactivism' posits that observers actively shape the worlds they perceive" (Tsaplina and Barfield 116). From this perspective, medical science authorizes only one view on reality to its detriment because "imagination is the origin of any hypothesis that leads to discovery … shining light into areas that are as yet dark to our understanding" (115). Tsaplina notes that a self, fractured through illness, already experiences a world made strange and enacts daily, hourly artistic solutions to the task of living. Such a fractured experience may be "reintegrated even if the physical condition does not leave. This is why a cure may not necessarily heal, and healing does not depend upon cure" (117). It does, however, depend on care, which she and Barfield describe as "a deeply imaginative act" (117) one in which those with "unique precarities" provide key insights (Tsaplina, Beitiks, and Huffman).

Sing, O Muse, of the Effects of Age

An octogenarian with soft white curls and glasses sits in a wheelchair in the center of a gray-beige carpeted ecumenical worship space, bearing a crocheted blanket on her lap and wearing a bright teal, broad-collared jacket of soft material. She hoists a copy of *The Odyssey* in steady, knotted hands and speaks loudly, "If the Gods will grant us a happier old age, we'll be free from our trials at last!" Behind her, a chorus of her peers, supported by younger interlocutors, extend and amplify her words until they fill the sanctuary. This is a moment from

The Penelope Project, woven by Professor Anne Basting (University of Wisconsin, Milwaukee) and many partners from similar strands of perseverance and patience as Penelope's never-quite-completed burial shroud.[19]

In her 2016 book *The Penelope Project: An Arts-Based Odyssey to Change Elder Care*, Basting offers a "practical manual, a manual of practice" for creating theater with older adults, though hers is not a "how to" book (Odendahl-James 605). Instead, she invites theater practitioners who engage health-care spaces focused on chronic and cognitive conditions of aging to come equipped with imagination and improvisation and insists they give her their most precious commodity – time. Basting employs her considerable facilitation skills in the organization of the book, sharing editorial credit, spotlighting the first-person stories of her collaborators as they craft an installation/durational theatrical performance based on Homer's *The Odyssey.* She presents an intensely dramaturgical story of *The Penelope Project*'s construction and intentions, not just because it boasts a foreword by one of the field's revered elders, Elinor Fuchs. Basting sets aside any efforts toward a chronicle of a final product[20] and places the multidimensional and multivocal three-year process center stage. Readers are privy to side conversations, research roads traveled and abandoned, and the navigation of hurdles when working in dissimilar disciplinary spaces, all while bearing the pressures of community stakeholders focused on health, care, and resources. She includes evidence of success from students, educators, and health-care professionals, although no evidence is perhaps more compelling than the fact that this account was published the very year (2016) Basting was awarded a MacArthur Fellowship to support her future work in creative research.

In the most recent evolution of her practice, Basting continues to center performing artists and their creative work as health-care-centered researchers, as their skills and purposes are complementary to but distinct from that of drama or art therapists. When medical science employs theater, researchers tend to measure its effectiveness under very particular definitions of patient or provider outcomes, and the artist's value in health studies is confirmed (or not) by the usefulness of arts practices to health-care practitioner, such as emotional connection, storytelling, improvisation, and vocal and physical dynamism (Odendahl-James 605). Basting flips this script, but she avoids casting the artist as the clinician's antagonist. Instead, she interrogates the latter's belief that their clinical training provides the skills required to meet the needs of geriatric patients, those with dementia and Alzheimer's especially. What artists do, and what theater artists do uniquely well, is "invite us into recognizing and being present with each other," a surrender of time, attention, and ego that is both critically necessary for the complex contours of elder care and a currently untapped capacity of many clinical practitioners working within the constraints of U.S. for-profit health-care systems (Basting, Towey, and Rose 163).

Charting Dementia's Unfolding Reality

For her 2020 book *Creative Care: A Revolutionary Approach to Dementia and Elder Care*, Basting continues her practice of sharing space and authority with those who carry lived experience of aging in senior centers, memory care programs, and residential facilities. Basting is one of a handful of theater scholars who has organized the potent but specific terms of her art into an expansive and compelling claim regarding strategies for ethical and effective care that are endorsed by medical practitioners without losing artistic nuance, experimentation, or challenge to rigid systems. Basting's presentation of creativity as accessible, infinitely adaptable, and not disciplinary specific seems key to its embrace by health-care providers. She potently pairs creativity with the idea of *care*, itself an idealized term in the arts and medicine:

> Creative care. It's more than medicine. It's more than the arts. It is more than therapy, but it has measurable therapeutic benefits… . Creative care is an agreement between people to imagine themselves, each other and their worlds a little differently. It is an invitation to shape the world together. For people denied the tools for world-shaping, this invitation can be a profound and life-changing act of healing.
>
> (Basting, *Creative Care* 57)

One can hear echoes of Tsaplina and Barfield's call for imagination as an essential tool for medical research in Basting's invitation. In *The Penelope Project*, Basting's work was supported by students in applied theater classrooms, individuals who were likely to exercise their theatrical training in domains outside of theater (e.g., in spheres like education, health, and civics). In *Creative Care*, theater artists are present, but their work provides the mise-en-scene for the evaluative expertise of psychologists, gerontologists, dementia and Alzheimer's researchers, and the first-person accounts of individuals and caregivers who have put into practice the tools and principles Basting describes.

Basting codified TimeSlips in 1998 as a set of practices and an entity of evaluation and introduces the term to a wider audience in her 2009 book *Forget Memory: Creating Better Lives for People with Dementia*. The growing body of TimeSlips clinical studies[21] demonstrates that creative practices and values have an impact on health outcomes. Anecdotal stories remain central to the work and continue to provide potent answers to Basting's initial questions about whether we can summon the will to change our "attitudes and our care practices" without waiting for science to provide what would only ever be provisional guidance (Basting, *Forget Memory* 3). In *Creative Care*, the tone is lighter than in *Forget Memory*, perhaps buoyed by a chorus of medical professionals who echo Basting's ideas. This new support might reflect new urgency. In the decade between Basting's two books, dementia has grown to be the fifth leading cause of death globally ("Towards a Dementia Plan" 6) with over 5.5 million Americans over 65 currently diagnosed with Alzheimer's dementia, a number anticipated to reach almost 14 million by 2050 (Alzheimer's Association, "Disease Facts and Figures"). In that time, TimeSlips has become a global brand, offering six values available to all who are willing:

1 Saying Yes, And
2 Asking Beautiful Questions
3 Giving Proof of Listening
4 Opening Ourselves to Wonder
5 Committing to rigor and the value of all human beings
6 Finding meaning by connecting our personal expressions to the larger world.

("Our Story")

While values 1, 3, and 4 will be familiar to those who have studied acting or improvisation, nothing in this list requires formal arts education. That said, skilled artisans and facilitators have shaped TimeSlips' materials and mechanisms for use by non-arts partners, be they medical or social, congregate living supporters or individual caregivers.

Asking Beautiful Questions

Creative Care is a dramaturgy primer for dementia caregivers, giving them tools to fashion meaning within a patient's world often described in medical literature as unknowable. Basting offers an idealized vision of engagement but one that does not deny the barriers its optimism might encounter. She gives validation and support for caregivers assumed to be engaging creative strategies whether they employ the structured (if open-ended) exercises proffered but always navigating days populated with challenges and moments of ease. Unwilling to wait for clinical research to agree on the acceptable degrees of quantitative change necessary for a treatment protocol, Basting places the authority for supportive health-care practices in the hands of artists, caregivers, empathetic staff, and progressive administrators. Here, I unpack the specific dramaturgical power of values 2 and 5 to illustrate how Basting shifts the grounds of "two cultures" collaboration to appeal directly to constituents of need, and how she carves out potential avenues for this work with potential future partners within disability justice and performance practice communities.

Value 2 sits tantalizingly close to the dramaturg's directive to ask probing questions. Basting describes the inspiration as a happy accident that emerged out of multiple weeks working in a retirement community with little success drawing out the residents. A hastily crafted question about what name to give the Marlboro Man resulted in an extended, animated conversation – one that helped her realize that although all questions are interrogative, not all are asked in optimal ways. Many might think of these as "open-ended" questions, but Basting insists on the idea of beauty. TimeSlips' workshops provide considered and tested questions that fashion art out of conversational data. Beauty represents a critical concept for conversations that have too often been presented as loss or diminishment; it represents a claim to presence and creation that is frequently denied dementia patients:

> To ask a beautiful question as an invitation to another is to believe that the listener can do this and that the asker will receive and honor the listener's answer. So the beautiful question is an invitation both to selfhood and to community simultaneously.
>
> (Basting, *Creative Care*, 76–77)

For Basting, beautiful questions are endlessly generative. When Basting or her collaborators ask these in workshops, they encourage listeners to free their responses from the "tyranny of memory."[22] Such questions circumvent the notion of a right or a wrong answer and allow for a dramaturgy in the moment versus a prescribed or anticipated narrative order. Facilitators coax participants to probe deeper not toward a known or common answer but toward language we discover together. Beautiful questions can revel in repetition, nonsense, and frivolity, making space for release and without self-doubt. No matter the participants' difference in status, the stakes are lowered and all are provided respite from struggles over meaning. While Basting's beautiful question protocol happens inside particular kinds of caregiving interactions, the experience and engagement it provides might unlock more options for openness in other contexts.

Time to Care

The term "disability" does not feature prominently in Basting's texts, an absence one might attribute to her efforts to shift narratives about aging away from limitation and deficit, associations that often accompany the word. There is, however, a strategic if unstated link between creative care value 5 – Committing to rigor and the value of all human beings – and principles of disability justice. In geriatrics, the general focus is on research into better outcomes, for a return to daily life after surgery and accidents and management of chronic conditions, and less a pursuit of cures.[23] In these efforts, medical collaborations with artists have focused on fostering "well-being," offering a range of embodied and creative experiences to mitigate the inevitable changes that accompany aging.[24] The shift away from curing cognitive conditions (from autism to Alzheimer's) has been an evolving process driven in no small part by the work of disability activists who have argued these conditions are not a failure of a nonfunctioning bodymind but offer wholly unique cognitive landscapes and modes of communication.[25]

Given the expanded and specific nature of dementia and Alzheimer's within elder/aging populations, Basting scales up arts interventions for older adult communities in ways that center artists' creative research. Unlike mainstream creativity or so-called brain-training apps or video games, TimeSlips is not a rehabilitation or arts therapy tool.[26] Rather, it is a set of interactions and intentions employing creativity at whatever level or under whatever conditions exist. Basting does not address disability justice head-on; instead, these principles are implied by her focus on time, improvisation, iteration, and the democratization of creativity. Elements of such practices are gaining ground as diagnoses rise in an aging population around the world. There are "memory towns" (Kotecki) and reminiscence therapy (Hurley), intergenerational living spaces (Jansen), and a few European villages where medical staff perform care as daily life in a town outfitted in the style and era aligned with its inhabitants' awareness (Planos).

In much of *Creative Care*, Basting shares basic tools and techniques to meet loved ones wherever they may be in their condition. She encourages a recalibration of time on three scales: individual, familial, and communal (which includes community care and institutional health spaces). I see this invitation as Basting's version of Alison Kafer's crip time,[27] offering caregivers and people in care a new connection. Her work enacts a disability justice modality by recognizing that accommodation requires shifting the grounds of time, communication, and visibility. Basting also argues, however indirectly, for dismantling the medical model of treatment by dismantling the medical model of evaluating health outcomes: "Double-blind, randomized control studies that have always been called the 'gold standard' in research will not always work to best capture the benefits of arts programming in care settings" (Basting, *Creative Care* 265). Whereas TimeSlips is available for use and assessment by health practitioners who provide Basting with evidence of effectiveness to support her pursuit of research funding, creative care practices represent subtle alternatives to quantitative evaluations. First, Basting offers these mechanisms to any individual who chooses to engage. Second, she shifts the significance of pursued outcomes from medical standards to individual and community engagement. Patients and their care teams can create their own evaluations to assess what TimeSlips strategies work and what value they place on them.

The notion of self-authorship is a privilege perhaps most associated with youth, a skill set that evolves as one meets each stage of life. When life's experiences confound linearity even as the years continue to advance, the approach to self-authorship necessarily needs and generates new dramaturgies. Referencing her own mother's Alzheimer's diagnosis, Basting notices the need for "strength to push beyond the grief over changes" seen in people we knew as one way before and "open hearts to help invite and reveal who the person is now" (Basting, *Creative Care* 265). TimeSlips invites us into dramaturgical relationship to these conditions, ones that may also come to us directly. The gods-granted "happier old age" is not one without trial but is one where we might recalibrate the terms of our struggles. To be "free from our trials" does not mean they do not exist but that we might meet them with community, creativity, and care.

Notes

1 This moment is reconstructed from my classroom discussion notes for September 8, 2021.

2 In his initial critique of Shepherd-Barr's *Science on Stage*, Djerassi cites her inclusion of *Angels in America* as evidence of a "idiosyncratic" definition of science (63).

3 The Geffen School of Medicine at UCLA has an arts analogue in the Geffen School of Drama at Yale.

4 Narratologist Jim Phelan's influence looms large in Charon's work.

5 See chapters 4 and 8 in *Principles and Practices of Narrative Medicine.*

6 Such a philosophy represents a precursor to "social prescribing," defined by a 2021 editorial in *eClinical Medicine* as "the formalized process by which primary care physicians either directly or indirectly link primary care patients with non-medical interventions which aim to reduce the burden of health-care concerns." Such nonmedical interventions include "art classes for wellbeing, knitting, singing, or walking groups."

7 See Howley, Gaufberg, and King particularly pages 17–19 for a discussion of arts and humanities programs (1991–2019) designed for health-care providers.

8 The Mayo Clinic has collaborated with the American Medical Association on longitudinal studies about physician burnout since the 2000s, reporting in 2016 that rates had reached a high of 55% compared to 28% for U.S. workers overall.

9 See Dean and Talbot for a discussion of "moral injury" as it applies to medicine.

10 In his analysis of empathy, Bloom mentions literary examples in passing but omits a deep dive into popular culture and media save for how these sources contribute to emotional empathy, which is the kind of empathy that he finds lacking and problematic in relationship to moral and social decision making, unlike Blank and Jensen.

11 Most of these programs consist of minors comprised of five to six courses.

12 As of this writing, only the University of Washington and Temple, Syracuse, and Ohio State Universities offer undergraduate degree credentials in the field of disability studies.

13 The italicized text reflects class notes I took during Tsaplina's workshop with visual cultures of medicine students at Duke University on April 10, 2019.

14 "Betes" is from the French for "beast," but the name is pronounced /beeteez/ to emulate the way many pronounce diabetes: /dahy-*uh*-bee-teez/.

15 As articulated by artists/scholars Terry Galloway, Donna Nudd, and Carrie Sandahl, "The Ethic of Accommodation means making room for differences possible, letting go of preconceived notions of perfectibility, and negotiating complex sets of needs… . The Ethic of Accommodation inspires creative aesthetic choices… . Practicing the ethic enhances theatrical practice" (229).

16 In their 2001 article for *Contemporary Theatre Review* about the forms and practices of Uppity Theatre's DisAbility Project, Joan Lipkin and Ann Fox note that their idea of "accessibility … doesn't just mean a level playing field, but indeed, an explosion of possibility; … an aesthetics of access that at once voices the experiences of persons with disabilities – while imagining beyond [current] boundaries" (136).

17 See Landry-Wegener et al. for a recent scoping review of medical journal databases regarding the use of these and other theater tools.

18 Tsaplina was influenced in this idea by medical anthropologists Margaret Lock and Nancy Scheper-Hughes and their construct of the individual body (the bodymind), the social body, and the political body all in active

resistance to medicine's insistence on a bodily whole and coherent consciousness.

19 The description of this scene is crafted from viewing the documentary *Penelope* (2011) created by Basting with director Brad Lichtenstein.

20 More scenes from the performance can be found in Lichtenstein's documentary available for rent on Vimeo.

21 See George et al. and Kim et al. for two examples written a decade apart.

22 This was a phrase used frequently at the Virtual Creative Care Institute I attended in 2020.

23 Atul Gawande's *Being Mortal* provides a broad overview of medicine's attitude toward the inevitable changes that come with older age, particularly chapter 3, "Dependence."

24 See Goldbard, particularly pages 15–17, which mention the work of both Tsaplina and Basting.

25 See, for instance, the work of Lydia X.Z. Brown (www.lydiaxzbrown.com/) and her early blog autistichoya.com.

26 See Simons.

27 In her book *Feminist, Queer, Crip*, Kafer describes "crip time" as "flex time not just expanded but exploded; it requires re-imagining our notions of what can and should happen in time or recognizing how expectations of 'how long things take' are based on very particular minds and bodies. Rather than bend disabled bodies and minds to meet the clock, crip time bends the clock to meet disabled bodies and minds" (27).

References

Alzheimer's Association. "2019 Alzheimer's Disease Facts and Figures Report." https://alz.org/media/Documents/alzheimers-facts-and-figures-2019-r.pdf.

Basting, Anne. *Creative Care: A Revolutionary Approach to Dementia and Elder Care.* Harper, 2020.

Basting, Anne. *Forget Memory: Creating Better Lives for People with Dementia.* Johns Hopkins University Press, 2009.

Basting, Anne, Maureen Towey, and Ellie Rose, editors. *The Penelope Project: An Arts-Based Odyssey to Change Elder Care.* University of Iowa Press, 2016.

Berg, Sara. "Half of Health Workers Report Burnout amid COVID-19." *American Medical Association*, 20 July 2021. ama-assn.org/practice-management/physician-health/half-health-workers-report-burnout-amid-covid-19.

Blank, Jessica, and Erik Jensen. "The Uses of Empathy: Theater and the Real World." *Theatre History Studies*, vol. 25, 2005, pp. 15–22.

Bloom, Paul. *Against Empathy: The Case for Rational Compassion.* HarperCollins, 2016.

Brecht, Bertolt. "A Short Organum for the Theatre." *Brecht on Theatre: The Development of an Aesthetic*, edited and translated by John Willett. Hill and Wang, 1984, pp. 172–205.

Charon, Rita. "Narrative Medicine: A Model for Empathy, Reflection, Profession, and Trust." *JAMA*, vol. 286, no. 15, 2001, pp. 1897–1902. doi:10.1001/jama.286.15.1897.

Charon, Rita, et al. The Principles and Practice of Narrative Medicine. *Oxford University Press, 2017.*

Clare, Eli. *Brilliant Imperfection: Grappling with Cure.* Duke University Press, 2017.

Couser, G. Thomas. "What Disability Studies Has to Offer Medical Education." *The Journal of Medical Humanities*, vol. 32, no. 1, 2011, pp. 21–30. doi:10.1007/s10912-010-9125-1.

Crawford, Paul, et al. *Health Humanities.* Palgrave Macmillan, 2015.

Dean, Wendy, and Simon G. Talbot. "Physicians Aren't 'Burning Out.' They're Suffering from Moral Injury." *STAT News*, 26 July 2018. www.statnews.com/2018/07/26/physicians-not-burning-out-they-are-suffering-moral-injury/.

Djerassi, Carl. "Review of *Science on Stage: From Doctor Faustus to Copenhagen* by Kirsten Shepherd-Barr." *Physics Today*, vol. 60, no. 2, 2007, pp. 63–64.

Epstein, Steven, and Stefan Timmermans. "From Medicine to Health: The Proliferation and Diversification of Cultural Authority." *Journal of Health and Social Behavior*, vol. 62, no. 3, Sept. 2021, pp. 240–254. doi:10.1177/00221465211010468.

Galloway, Terry, Donna Marie Nudd, and Carrie Sandahl. "'Actual Lives' and the Ethic of Accommodation." *The Community Performance Reader*, edited by Petra Kuppers and G. Robertson. Routledge, 2007, pp. 227–234.

Gawande, Atul. *Being Mortal: Medicine and What Matters in the End.* Metropolitan Books, 2014.

George, Daniel R., et al. *"Impact of Participation in TimeSlips, a Creative Group-Based Storytelling Program, on Medical Student Attitudes toward Persons with Dementia: A Qualitative Study."* The Gerontologist*, vol. 51, no. 5, 2011, pp. 699–703. doi:10.1093/geront/gnr035.*

Goldbard, Arlene. *Art & Well-Being: Toward a Culture of Health.* U.S. Department of Arts and Culture, 2018.

Howley, Lisa, Elizabeth Gaufberg, and Brandy Kin. *FRAME: The Fundamental Role of the Arts and Humanities in Medical Education.* AAMC, 2020.

Hurley, Amanda Kolson. "Time-Travel Therapy. Can a Faux 1950s Downtown Sharpen the Minds of Dementia Patients?" *The Atlantic*, Jan. 2017. theatlantic.com/magazine/ archive/2017/01/time-travel-therapy/508787/.

Jansen, Tiffany R. "The Nursing Home That's Also a Dorm." *Bloomberg News*, 2 Oct. 2015. bloomberg.com/news/articles/2015-2010-02/a-nursing-home-that-s-also-a-college-dorm.

Kafer, Alison. *Feminist, Queer, Crip.* Indiana University Press, 2013.

Kim, Seoyoun, et al. *"Generativity in Creative Storytelling: Evidence from a Dementia Care Community."* Innovation in Aging*, vol. 4, no. 2, 2020, pp. 1–7. doi:10.1093/geroni/igaa002.*

Kotecki, Peter. "Fake 1950s-Era Towns Are Popping Up Across the U.S. to Help Dementia Patients." *Business Insider*, 8 Oct. 2018.

Lamb, Erin, Sarah L. Berry, and Therese Jones. *Health Humanities Baccalaureate Programs in the United States and Canada*. case.edu/medicine/bioethics/education/health-humanities.

Landry-Wegener, Bernard, et al. *"Drama Training as a Tool to Teach Medical Trainees Communication Skills: A Scoping Review."* Academic Medicine, *vol. 98, no. 7, 2023, pp. 851–860. ovidsp.ovid.com/ovidweb.cgi?T=JS&PAGE=reference&D=ovftz&NEWS=N&AN=00001888-202307000-00038.*

Lichtenstein, Brad, Director. *Penelope: The Documentary*. 371 Productions, 2014. On Demand. Vimeo. 2015.

Lipkin, Joan, and Ann Fox. "The Disability Project: Toward an Aesthetic of Access." *Contemporary Theatre Review*, vol. 11, nos. 3–4, 2001, pp. 119–136.

Lorenz, Karl A., M. Jillisa Steckart, and Kenneth E. Rosenfeld. "End-of-Life Education Using the Dramatic Arts: The *Wit* Educational Initiative." *Academic Medicine*, vol. 79, no. 5, 2004, pp. 481–486. doi:10.1097/00001888-200405000-00020.

Mol, Annemarie. *The Logic of Care: Health and the Problem of Patient Choice*. Routledge, 2008.

Odendahl-James, Jules. "Review of *The Penelope Project: An Arts-Based Odyssey to Change Elder Care*, ed. by Anne Basting, Maureen Towey, Ellie Rose, and *Theatre for Children in Hospital: The Gift of Compassion* by Persephone Sextou." *Theatre Journal*, vol. 69, no. 4, 2017, pp. 604–606.

"Our Story." TimeSlips Inc. 2019. timeslips.org/about/our-story.

Palmer, Janice, and Florence Nash. *The Hospital Arts Handbook: A Resource Book for Arts and Humanities Programs in Health Care Settings*. Duke University Medical Center, 1991.

"Performing the Art of Medicine." *Total Art Journal*, vol. 1, no. 1, 2011. totalartjournal.com/.

Planos, Josh. "The Dutch Village Where Everyone Has Dementia." *The Atlantic*, 14 Nov. 2014. theatlantic.com/health/archive/2014/11/the-dutch-village-where-everyone-has-dementia/382195/.

Reddy, Sumathi. "A Prescription of Poetry to Help Patients Speak Their Minds: Doctors at Several Major Hospitals Are Experimenting with Poems as a Source of Psychological Relief and Connection." *Wall Street Journal*, 1 Dec. 2019. https://www.proquest.com/newspapers/prescription-poetry-help-patients-speak-their/docview/2320050453/se-2.

Rothenberg, Karen H., and Lynn W. Bush. "Manipulating Fate: Medical Innovations, Ethical Implications, Theatrical Illuminations." *Houston Journal of Health Law & Policy*, vol. 13, no. 1, Apr. 2012, pp. 1–77. search.ebscohost.com/login.aspx?direct=true&db=lft&AN=87756597&site=ehost-live&scope=site.

Scheper-Hughes, Nancy, and Margaret M. Lock. "The Mindful Body: A Prolegomenon to Future Work in Medical Anthropology." *Medical Anthropology Quarterly*, vol. 1, no. 1, 1987, pp. 6–41. jstor.org/stable/648769.

Simons, Daniel J., et al. "Do 'Brain-Training' Programs Work?" *Psychological Science in the Public Interest: A Journal of the American Psychological Society*, vol., 17, no. 3, 2016, pp. 103–186. doi:10.1177/1529100616661983.

"Social Prescribing: Addressing Societies' Holistic Health-Care Needs." *EclinicalMedicine*, Dec. 2021. doi:10.1016/j.eclinm.2021.101243.

Sweet, Cheryl A. "Movie 'Wit' Is a Hit with Medical Students Learning about Care of Dying Patients." Robert Wood Johnson Foundation, 10 Feb. 2007.

Tait, D. Shanafelt, et al. "Changes in Burnout and Satisfaction with Work-Life Balance in Physicians and the General U.S. Working Population Between 2011 and 2014." *Mayo Clinic Proceedings*, vol. 90, no. 12, 2015, pp. 1600–1613. doi:10.1016/j.mayocp.2015.08.023.

TimeSlips' Virtual Creative Care Institute. Zoom event, 15–16 July 2020.

"Towards a Dementia Plan: A WHO Guide." World Health Organization, 2018.

Tsaplina, Marina. "Bodies Speaking: Embodiment, Illness and the Poetic Materiality of Puppetry/Object Practice." *Journal of Applied Arts & Health*, vol. 11, no. 1–2, 2020, pp. 85–102.

Tsaplina, Marina. "Puppetry and Disability Aesthetics." *HowlRound.com*, 4 May 2020. howlround.com/puppetry-and-disability-aesthetics.

Tsaplina, Marina, and Raymond Barfield. "The Role of the Imagination in the Practices of the Health Humanities." *The Routledge Companion to Health Humanities*, edited by Paul Crawford, Brian Brown, and Andrea Charise. Routledge, 2020, pp. 111–119.

Tsaplina, Marina, Meghan Moe Beitiks, and Charlee Huffman. "Performing Public Health: Unique Precarities." *Creative Healthy Communities: Arts + Public Health in America*, 2020. arts.ufl.edu/sites/creating-healthy-communities/covid-19-arts-response/unique-precarities/.

Tsaplina, Marina, Jules Odendahl-James, and Torry Bend. "Attending to the 'Illusion of Life': Reimagining Medicine Through the Art of Puppetry Practice." *Puppetry International*, no. 44, 2018, pp. 16–19.

Index

For Product Safety Concerns and Information please contact our EU representative GPSR@taylorandfrancis.com
Taylor & Francis Verlag GmbH, Kaufingerstraße 24, 80331 München, Germany

www.ingramcontent.com/pod-product-compliance
Lightning Source LLC
LaVergne TN
LVHW010948110826
845149LV00015B/3263

* 9 7 8 1 0 3 2 7 9 0 2 3 7 *